One Flesh: A Testimony of Marriage and God's Intervention

Author: Nathan Martinichio

Contents

Introduction 3
Testimony Summary 6
One Flesh 23
Personal pursuit of Jesus 32
Live in Truth 40
Surrendering and Humility 46
Child Rearing 53
If I Could Change One Thing 61
Conclusion 70

Introduction

I'm excited to share with you the purpose and backstory behind this book because it holds deep personal significance for me. Ever since I was a child, I've had a creative spark that seemed to burn constantly within me. I loved drawing, telling elaborate stories, and immersing myself in make-believe worlds. As I entered my teenage years, my passion for books grew, and I discovered the incredible depth and boundless creativity they offered. I was fascinated by the worlds they opened and the wisdom they contained. Little did I know that during this time, my interest in the human mind and how it worked—psychology—was also quietly taking shape in the background.

Psychology is a mind-blowing field of study because, despite what society might lead you to believe, it isn't just a dry scientific discipline. It unveils the awe-inspiring complexity of God's thoughts woven into His creation. Through studying the intricacies of human behavior, emotions, and cognition, I came to see how beautifully we are "fearfully and wonderfully made" (Psalm 139:14, NASB). Psychology reveals the deep intricacies of God's design and points to His intentional creation. And as I'll explain in the next chapter, psychology actually played a pivotal role in leading me to salvation.

As my fascination with books and psychology grew, so did my dream of writing. I always had this grand vision of writing an amazing book—one that could rival the bestsellers. But I wasn't interested in writing a typical non-fiction "self-help" book. I craved something intensely creative—maybe a mind-bending science fiction tale or a gripping mix of action and mystery. I even tried a few times and managed to crank out around 70 to 80 pages at one point. But then something happened—burnout set in. What had started with excitement and passion turned into a monotonous chore. The drive and vision I once had faded, and my interest died out altogether.

You might be wondering how all of this connects to marriage and Jesus, the focal points of this book. That's a great question! See, as Christians, we often discover that pursuing endeavors outside of God's will inevitably leads to failure. When I look back, I realize that those writing projects failed because I was pursuing them in my own strength. I had forgotten to ask the most important question: "Is this part of God's plan for me?"

Perhaps you can relate. Have you ever started a project or pursued a goal that seemed right at the time, only to realize later that it wasn't aligned with what God had planned for you? Maybe you experienced burnout, disappointment, or even failure. It's a hard lesson, but sometimes we need to let go of what we think is best and surrender to what God knows is best. Proverbs 3:5-6 (NASB) speaks directly to this:
"Trust in the Lord with all your heart, and do not lean on your own understanding. In all your ways acknowledge Him, and He will make your paths straight."

Let me be real with you—I don't have fancy degrees or formal education in psychology, marriage, or theology. So, why on earth would I dare to write a book centered around these topics? Well, here's an important lesson I've learned: The world calls those who are ordained, but God ordains those who are called. This has been a guiding truth in my life. It reminds me of how God often chooses unlikely people to carry out His purposes. He isn't bound by human qualifications or credentials. As 1 Corinthians 1:27 says, "God has chosen the foolish things of the world to shame the wise, and God has chosen the weak things of the world to shame the things which are strong" (NASB).

My wife and I have a testimony that many would consider incredible—an account of how God not only saved us but restored and healed our brokenness, bringing us into deep reconciliation with Him. Those close to us have caught glimpses of our story. One day, a coworker remarked on how perfect our marriage seemed. I gently corrected them, explaining that perfection wasn't the right word to describe our relationship. Our marriage had been forged through overcoming extremely challenging and dark times. Intrigued, my coworker asked how we managed to overcome those difficulties. I began sharing a snippet of our testimony, accompanied by one of the vital truths that God had revealed to us in the context of our marriage—a truth that would later be discussed in this book.

After talking for about half an hour, I realized I had gone down the rabbit hole and apologized for taking up so much time. I casually mentioned that I could talk about these things for hours, to which my coworker responded, "And I would listen." This unexpected comment stirred something within me. They even suggested I write a book about our experiences so they could read it.

Initially, I dismissed the idea. After all, I had tried writing books before and failed. If I were to write a book, it would have to compete with the bestsellers out there—how foolish and arrogant of me to think that way. Yet, I couldn't shake the feeling that maybe, just maybe, I was supposed to write this book. Why was this bothering me so much? After all, I lacked the qualifications and credentials that would lend credibility to such a work.

Then, in a moment of clarity, the Holy Spirit reminded me of a profound truth—God's plans are not always aligned with our own, and His ways far surpass our understanding (Isaiah 55:8-9, NASB). I realized that God ordains those He calls, regardless of human qualifications. His authority extends over every aspect of life—including psychology, marriage, and theology. It wasn't my job to meticulously plan every detail of our testimony or its impact. It was His divine will. My role was to surrender and trust Him to do the work.

You see, surrendering to God's plan requires letting go of our own ideas of success, control, and timing. It's not always easy, especially when we have our own dreams or when we've invested so much into something that doesn't turn out the way we expected. But I've learned that God's plan is always better. When we surrender, we find that He leads us down paths we could never have imagined. Psalm 37:5 (NASB) says, "Commit your way to the Lord, trust also in Him, and He will do it."

So, here I am—surrendering to the Creator—and embarking on the daunting task of writing a book that I initially believed was beyond my capabilities. But now I understand that it's not about my capabilities; it's about what God can do through me. May God bless this endeavor, and may those who read these pages be enriched and blessed by His words.

Galatians 2:20 (NASB)
"I have been crucified with Christ; and it is no longer I who live, but Christ lives in me; and the life which I now live in the flesh I live by faith in the Son of God, who loved me and gave Himself up for me."

Testimony Summary

At the tender age of 16, I crossed paths with the woman who would eventually become my wife. She happened to be an acquaintance of a close friend, so when I laid eyes on her, initiating a conversation felt as natural as breathing. There was no hesitation, no awkwardness—just a sense that meeting her was somehow meant to happen. Our first encounter took place at a youth club, a space specifically designed for teenagers. It had the energy of a lively social scene, a place where the music was always pumping and the room buzzed with excitement. It was a setting designed to help teens unwind and connect, and that's exactly what we did.

From the moment we met, a powerful connection seemed to spark between us. It wasn't just a fleeting attraction—it felt as if we had known each other for years, as though we were picking up a conversation that had been paused for only a moment. There was a deep sense of comfort and familiarity, which I now see as one of the many ways God begins weaving our lives together, even when we don't fully recognize His hand in the process.

That night, we were inseparable. Every minute we spent together only deepened the bond that was forming. It was as though time stood still, and the rest of the world faded into the background. We laughed, shared stories, and found ourselves locked in conversation that felt far more meaningful than what you'd expect from two teenagers meeting for the first time. It was effortless, a flow that hinted at something bigger than just a casual meeting.

By the end of that evening, it was clear to both of us that this was the beginning of something special. We parted reluctantly, but even when we couldn't be together physically, we found other ways to remain close. We spent countless hours on the phone, talking deep into the night. Those conversations stretched on for what seemed like eternity—neither of us wanted them to end. We shared our dreams, our fears, and everything in between. We were building a foundation of communication that, unbeknownst to us at the time, would serve us well through the many highs and lows of our relationship.

Looking back now, I can't help but marvel at how God orchestrated these moments, even though we didn't see it then. At 16, I didn't know what the future held, but God did. Even in those simple, innocent moments of getting to know each other, He was laying the groundwork for a lifelong partnership—one that would be tested, refined, and ultimately restored through His grace. Sometimes, we think we are in control of the story we're writing, but God, in His infinite wisdom, is the true Author, guiding our steps long before we even realize it.

However, being young and dumb and outside the will of God, we were having sex outside of marriage which led to us becoming pregnant at the young age of 17. United by a profound love for each other, we shared a common desire to start a family. At the time, our longing was pure, but our understanding of the responsibilities that came with parenthood was limited at best. We were young—just 17—and, like many teenagers, we believed that love alone was enough to see us through the challenges ahead. It was a beautiful but naïve notion, one that didn't account for the practical realities of life. We were driven by emotion and the idea of building something together, but we didn't fully grasp the weight of what it meant to raise a child or the sacrifices required to create a stable life.

Recognizing the pressing need for stability, particularly in terms of healthcare and financial security, we quickly realized that our youthful passion wasn't enough. We needed a plan. The worldly pressures to provide for a family began to settle heavily on my shoulders, and I knew I had to make a decision that would provide for us. **But at 17, options were scarce.** Without much formal education or work experience, the paths available to me were limited. After weighing what few options I had, I decided to join the military.

Joining the military seemed like the most practical solution. It provided immediate benefits—a steady income, healthcare, and a sense of stability—all things we desperately needed. It didn't require an advanced skillset or higher education beyond obtaining a GED, and once we were officially married, my wife and our future children would be entitled to healthcare benefits. In many ways, this decision was driven by necessity, but it also felt like an opportunity—a way for us to embark on a journey that would shape our lives in ways we couldn't fully comprehend at the time. **What I didn't know then was that this decision would also lead me down a path of personal struggles, transformation, and, ultimately, redemption.**

When it came time to propose to my wife, there were no extravagant gestures or elaborate surprises. There was no hidden ring, no meticulously planned moment. I hadn't arranged a candlelit dinner or orchestrated any grand romantic gesture. In fact, the moment was incredibly simple—perhaps too simple for such an important question. But in that simplicity, there was sincerity. One night, without any preamble, I casually turned to her and asked, "Will you marry me?"

I can still remember the look on her face—the way her eyes lit up with joy and her smile grew wide. **Overwhelmed with sheer delight**, she responded with an enthusiastic "yes." It wasn't the kind of proposal you see in movies, but for us, it was perfect. That moment was filled with the giddy excitement of two young people in love, ready to take on the world together. It may not have been wrapped in grandeur, but it sealed our commitment to spend the rest of our lives together. **Little did we know that the road ahead would be filled with challenges and growth, but at that moment, we were simply two people bound by love and the hope for a shared future.**

Our wedding day wasn't the result of meticulous planning or choosing a meaningful date for sentimental reasons. In fact, it was driven entirely by circumstance. **Christmas Eve**, a date most would select for its warmth and festive spirit, became our wedding day simply because it was the only available date when I returned from basic training during my military service. Timing wasn't on our side, and neither was circumstance. We had little control over the events that led up to that day, and yet, there was something beautifully simple and sincere about it.

There was no large gathering, no elaborate decorations or grand venue. Instead, with just our mothers as witnesses, we exchanged vows in a modest and intimate setting at the county magistrate's office. There was no extravagance, no fancy celebrations—just two young people deeply in love, ready to commit to each other for life. **What our wedding lacked in grandeur, it made up for in heart.** The simplicity of the moment allowed us to focus on what truly mattered—our love and the beginning of our shared journey.

Looking back, that day marked the start of something much larger than either of us could have imagined. Though the setting was humble, there was a profound sense of hope in the air. We were full of dreams, but unaware of the challenges that lay ahead. What we couldn't see at the time was how God would later work in our marriage, refining us through trials, healing the brokenness that we didn't even realize was already starting to form.

Behind the joy of our wedding day, there was a storm brewing beneath the surface—one I wasn't fully prepared to deal with. Growing up in an abusive household had a profound impact on my psychological well-being, shaping me in ways I hadn't yet come to understand. The pain, anger, and unresolved trauma I carried from my childhood followed me into adulthood, leading to irrational thought patterns and unhealthy coping mechanisms. Rather than confronting my past, I sought to escape it. Prior to joining the military, that escape often took the form of whatever substances were readily available, anything that could numb the emotional pain I didn't know how to process.

When I enlisted in the military, I had to leave behind some of those habits—at least the ones that involved drugs. The military's stringent drug testing policies during the entry process and throughout my service meant I couldn't continue down that path. **But I found another way to numb the pain—alcohol.** Despite being underage, my military affiliation made it easier for me to obtain alcohol. Being an active-duty service member seemed to grant me certain unspoken privileges, and few people were willing to refuse me.

Unfortunately, what started as a way to take the edge off quickly spiraled out of control. **I wasn't just drinking to relax—I was drinking to escape.** The emotional wounds I carried were never far from the surface, and alcohol became my way of pushing them down, even if only temporarily.

But like any temporary solution, it couldn't last. The more I drank, the more I lost control—not just of myself, but of my marriage.

The military life added to the strain. Long periods of separation due to training commitments only made things worse. My wife, at just 18, was left to navigate the challenges of young motherhood alone, living in a modest apartment and trying to hold things together while I was away. I, on the other hand, struggled to remain faithful. The temptations of the world were constantly pulling me in different directions, and my commitment to our marriage began to falter.

We became caught in a destructive cycle. On the surface, we were still trying to make things work, but underneath, we were both hurting. **The demands of parenthood, the pressures of military life, and the weight of my unresolved past were all converging**, creating cracks in the foundation of our marriage. We were overwhelmed by the world's temptations and desires, and neither of us had the tools or the wisdom to navigate through them.

Eventually, we reached a breaking point. While I was still serving in the military, we decided to separate. It felt like the only option at the time. Our love had been strong, but the weight of everything we were facing seemed insurmountable. The life we had envisioned, the dreams we had shared—it all seemed to be slipping away, and we didn't know how to stop it.

Upon my discharge from the military, there was a small glimmer of hope that maybe we could reconcile and repair the damage that had been done. **We tried—**we truly did. Both of us wanted to believe that the love we had for each other could overcome the deep cracks that had formed in our marriage. We attempted to work through our issues, to communicate and reconnect, but it quickly became apparent that love alone wasn't enough. There were too many unresolved wounds, too many layers of hurt that had been left unaddressed.

Regrettably, our efforts fell short. My personal problems ran deeper than I realized, and my destructive behavior continued. Despite wanting to change, I found myself still drawn to the allure of the world. The temporary pleasures it offered—things that provided quick fixes for my internal struggles—were hard to resist. It's easy to give in to what feels good in the moment when you haven't dealt with the deeper pain inside. Consequently, we ended up separating once again, both of us heartbroken but unsure how to overcome the challenges we faced.

After a series of reckless decisions and unfortunate events, I found myself entangled in legal trouble. **The choices I made caught up with me**, leading to my arrest and subsequent sentencing to six months in prison. In some ways, it felt like rock bottom, but as I look back now, I see that God was already working through those circumstances.

Reflecting on that chapter of my life, I can confidently say that my time behind bars was both the **best and worst experience** I've ever had. On one hand, being in prison was isolating, humiliating, and filled with regret. But on the other hand, it forced me to confront myself in ways I never had before. Prior to my incarceration, I had burned bridges with nearly everyone in my life. I had no one left—no support system, no one to confide in. **I was alone.**

Yet, in that isolation, something unexpected happened. It was within those prison walls, cut off from the world, that I stumbled upon a passion for psychology. It wasn't something I had sought out intentionally; it was born out of necessity. **I had to understand myself**, to figure out why I was so deeply broken and what had driven me to this point. Psychology gave me a framework to begin analyzing my thoughts and behaviors, even if I didn't know what I was ultimately searching for at the time.

During this period, I was mentally and emotionally in shambles. The weight of everything I had done, combined with the trauma I had carried from my childhood, left me feeling like I was in a constant state of inner chaos. The person I had become was a far cry from who I had hoped to be, and I didn't see a way out. I had reached a disheartening conclusion: upon my release, my life would likely spiral into tragedy within a year. The future felt bleak, and the scenarios that played out in my mind weren't ones of redemption—they were ones of further destruction.

In my darkest moments, I envisioned three possible outcomes: engaging in reckless behavior that could lead to my death, succumbing fully to a self-destructive cycle of substance abuse, or contemplating the unthinkable act of ending my own life. But none of these options held any appeal. I didn't want to die. **I wanted to change.** But I had no idea how to begin.

It wasn't enough to simply say, "I will do better." Change required more than that. It required a complete transformation, a willingness to confront the deepest, darkest parts of myself and articulate the specific areas in need of improvement. I had to delve deeper than ever before. For the first time in my life, I realized that change couldn't be surface-level—it had to come from within, and it had to be real. **But how?**

My journey toward transformation didn't happen overnight. It wasn't a sudden epiphany that everything would be okay. Instead, it began with a simple yet difficult act—**articulating my emotions.** For the first time, I was forced to face the mess I had become, and the emotions I had buried deep began to rise to the surface. It all started with a single statement: "**I am angry.**"

At first, that was all I could identify—anger. But I knew I had to go deeper. I had to unravel where this anger came from, layer by layer, until I reached the root cause. So I began asking myself, "**Why?**"

Why was I angry?
Because I was stuck in prison.
Why was I in prison?
Because I did something stupid.
Why did I do something stupid?
Because I was drunk.
Why was I drunk?
Because I had a bad childhood and never learned to cope.
Why did my childhood hurt so much?
Because my mother was abusive and refused to acknowledge my pain.
Why did her refusal to acknowledge my pain still affect me?
Because I cannot feel whole unless she acknowledges it and takes responsibility.
Why?
Because the pain she inflicted on me still holds power over my life, and I've allowed it to dictate my choices.
Why have I allowed it to control me?

Because I'm using the pain from my past as a justification for the destructive decisions I'm making today.

It was through this relentless questioning that I began to unravel the layers of my emotions and the complex web of behaviors that had shaped my life. I realized that my anger wasn't just about being in prison—it went much deeper than that. **It was about unaddressed wounds from my past, unresolved trauma, and the ways I had allowed that pain to define me.** I had carried the weight of my childhood for so long that it had become an integral part of my identity. But in doing so, I had given that pain far too much power.

The process of peeling back those layers wasn't easy. Each new "why" forced me to confront painful memories, uncomfortable truths, and parts of myself I had long avoided. But it was a necessary step toward healing. **I had to face the reality that the person most responsible for my pain was not someone else—it was me.**

As I continued this journey of introspection, a sobering truth began to emerge: **I was the root cause of every negative emotion and conflict in my life.** My choices, my reactions, my failure to address my past—they were all factors in my own downfall. While it was easy to point fingers at my upbringing, my circumstances, or the people who had wronged me, the truth was that I had made choices. And those choices had led me here.

This realization was both liberating and terrifying. On one hand, it meant that I had the power to change my life. On the other hand, it meant that I had to take full responsibility for my actions. I couldn't blame my past or my pain anymore. **I was the problem.**

But realizing that I was the problem presented an even greater challenge: **How does someone, who is the source of their own problems, stop creating more?** How do you break the cycle when you're the one perpetuating it? This was the question that haunted me. I knew I needed to change, but I didn't know how to begin. The weight of my own failures was heavy, and the task of fundamentally changing who I was seemed impossible.

It became clear to me that I couldn't do it alone. **The truth is, no one can.** When you've spent years entangled in destructive habits and thinking patterns, it's nearly impossible to dig yourself out without help. I had reached the end of myself, and I knew that real transformation—lasting change—would require something outside of my own willpower or strength.

I realized that if I was going to truly change, I needed an external force—**a power greater than myself**—to intervene. My very existence depended on it. But where would that help come from? I had searched in all the wrong places—substances, temporary pleasures, unhealthy relationships—and none of them had filled the void. It was then, in the depths of my despair, that I began to consider the possibility of something greater.

In my search for answers, I explored various avenues. I turned to **Scientology**, intrigued by its promise of self-realization and spiritual enlightenment. But as I delved into its teachings, I found it to be cold and distant, more about controlling behavior than addressing the deep wounds of the soul. It didn't offer the personal connection or sense of grace I was searching for.

Next, I explored the realms of **quantum physics**, hoping that science could explain the nature of existence and provide the answers to my inner turmoil. While it opened my eyes to the complexities of the universe, it left me feeling more insignificant and lost. The vastness of the cosmos only made my personal struggles feel more trivial, and the theoretical nature of it all didn't resonate with my heart. I needed something that would speak directly to my pain, not just intellectual curiosities.

I even briefly immersed myself in **Hinduism**, attracted to its ancient wisdom and the idea of karma. But as I studied it further, I realized that it, too, didn't offer the grace and forgiveness I so desperately needed. It emphasized actions and consequences but didn't provide a way to break free from the cycle of guilt and shame that had plagued my life.

After exhausting these avenues, I felt more lost than ever. **None of these pursuits offered a solution that resonated with my soul.** It was as though

I had opened door after door, only to find them all leading to dead ends. **It was then, in a last-ditch effort, that I turned to Jesus.**

At first, the simplicity of salvation through Jesus seemed almost too easy. **Acknowledge Jesus as God? Repent of my sins? No additional works or rituals?** It felt overly simplistic and, in my skeptical mind, somewhat insincere. Could transformation really be that straightforward? Could forgiveness and grace truly be extended without me having to earn it? These were questions I wrestled with, but deep down, I knew I had nothing left to lose. My life depended on finding something real, something that could bring about the change I so desperately sought.

In a moment of surrender, I decided to **open my heart to the possibility of Jesus.** Even though it felt unfamiliar and uncertain, I realized that none of my previous efforts had worked, and I was running out of time.

During my time in prison, I was invited by a fellow inmate to attend a **church service**. While I can't recall the exact words of the sermon, I remember that it stirred something inside me. It didn't hit me like a lightning bolt, but it was enough to soften my heart, enough to plant a seed of curiosity. For the first time, I felt something I hadn't felt in a long time—**hope**. It wasn't loud or overwhelming, but it was there, gently pulling at the edges of my heart.

Later that night, I returned to my sleeping area with a restless mind. Something had shifted in me during that service, but I couldn't quite put my finger on it. I picked up a Bible, not entirely sure where to start. For reasons I still can't explain, I felt drawn to the **book of Romans**. Perhaps it was divine intervention, or maybe it was just a random choice—but looking back, I believe God was leading me to the very words I needed to hear.

I devoured the book of Romans in one sitting. **Chapter after chapter**, I was confronted with the reality of sin, grace, and salvation. By the time I reached **Romans 10**, where it says, "If you confess with your mouth Jesus as Lord, and believe in your heart that God raised Him from the dead, you will be saved" (Romans 10:9, NASB), I knew something had shifted in me. The words felt alive, speaking directly to my heart. It wasn't just a story on the page—it was the truth, and it was gripping me in a way I hadn't expected.

Despite the tug I felt, I stayed reserved, unsure if I was ready to fully surrender. But those words—**God's words—**echoed in my mind long after I closed the Bible. That night, I tried to sleep, but I couldn't. The message from Romans, the hope of salvation, and the offer of grace repeated in my head like a song I couldn't shake.

Eventually, I got up to use the restroom, unable to quiet the unrest in my heart. But I didn't make it all the way there. **As I approached the entrance to the community restroom in that federal prison, I fell to my knees.** I had reached the end of myself, the end of running, and in that moment, I couldn't hold back the flood of emotions any longer. **I began to weep.**

I poured my heart out to Jesus, confessing everything—all the pain, the mistakes, the hurt I had caused others and myself. I told Him everything because I had nothing left to hide, no more masks to wear, no more excuses to give. **In that moment, I placed my life in His hands.** It wasn't just a simple prayer or a quick decision—it was the moment my life was forever changed. I had finally surrendered, and for the first time in my life, I felt what it was like to be truly free.

Having found salvation just three weeks before my release from prison, I felt a sense of hope and renewal. But that hope was quickly accompanied by a daunting reality. **I had burned all my bridges.** There was no one to call, no place to stay, no support system waiting for me outside those prison walls. The weight of that truth hit me hard as my release date approached. I was stepping into a world where I had no safety net and no clear path forward.

When the day of my release arrived, the prison system provided me with just enough money to get by for a short while—barely enough to cover food and transportation. They dropped me off at the nearest bus station in an unfamiliar city, where I was supposed to catch a bus back to my hometown. It all felt surreal—here I was, a free man in a world that now seemed foreign and intimidating.

I missed my bus by a mere ten minutes. **Ten minutes.** It felt like a cruel twist of fate, as if everything was conspiring to keep me from moving forward. In that moment, panic began to set in. I was alone, disoriented, and fearful of what would happen next. I didn't know where to go or what to do. All I could do was approach the clerk at the bus station, hoping for some guidance. Thankfully, they were kind enough to renew my ticket for the following day, but this presented a new problem: **where would I stay that night?**

With nowhere to turn, I began to search for help. I reached out to a local church and the Salvation Army, desperately hoping that someone could provide a temporary solution. By God's grace, I was directed to a nearby homeless shelter. But walking into that shelter was unlike anything I had ever experienced. **It felt alien, unfamiliar, and intimidating.** My heart was racing with uncertainty as I explained my situation to the staff.

Graciously, they extended a hand of help. They offered me a place to sleep for the night, food to eat, and even set an alarm to ensure I wouldn't miss my bus the next morning. For the first time since my release, I felt a sense of relief, albeit fragile. The pieces seemed to be falling into place.

But as I was beginning to relax, **another obstacle arose**. That night, the shelter experienced a brief power outage. It seemed like such a minor thing, but it was enough to reset the alarm clock that had been set for me. The next morning, I woke up to the sinking realization that **I had missed my bus again**. My heart sank as I processed what had happened. The panic from the day before returned in full force, and once again, I found myself back at square one.

Determined not to give up, I returned to the bus station and obtained yet another ticket for the following day. This time, the shelter worker, understanding the gravity of my situation, used their personal cellphone as an alarm to ensure I wouldn't miss the bus again. Everything seemed to be in place, and I allowed myself to believe that things might finally work out.

But then, **the morning came**, and with it, another unexpected setback. As the shelter staff and I tried to locate the worker who held the keys to access everyone's belongings, we found ourselves at a standstill. The worker with the keys was nowhere to be found. We waited, frantically searching for any way to retrieve my things, but our efforts were in vain. **By the time we realized it was too late, the bus had already left.**

It was as though the universe was testing me, throwing obstacle after obstacle in my path. **Each missed bus felt like another door slamming shut, another delay in the journey I so desperately wanted to take.** I couldn't help but question why all of this was happening, even as I tried to cling to the newfound faith I had discovered in Christ.

Standing in the parking lot of the shelter, I was filled with anger and frustration—not just at the situation, but at God. **Why was this happening?** I had surrendered my life to Him, yet everything seemed to be going wrong. In that moment of desperation, I did something I hadn't done before: I spoke to God audibly, right there in the open. It wasn't a calm prayer or a quiet reflection—it was a raw, emotional conversation. I pleaded with God, trying to convince Him that I needed to go home, that I couldn't take any more setbacks.

"Why are You letting this happen? I'm trying to change! I'm trying to do the right thing—why aren't You helping me?"

I didn't expect an answer, but I was desperate for one. **In the midst of my frustration, God provided a different kind of answer.** As I stood there pouring out my heart, a man from the shelter who had overheard my conversation approached me. He told me about the shelter's chapel, which was open for twelve hours each day. He mentioned a program they offered to help people deepen their relationship with Jesus, providing not only spiritual support but also assistance with housing and other needs.

Something stirred within me—**could this be the reason I was still here?** Could this shelter, this place that had seemed like just another setback, actually be part of God's plan for me?

Intrigued by the possibility, I made my way to the chapel and spoke with the chaplains. What I discovered changed the course of my journey. They offered an incredible program designed to help individuals not only survive but **thrive** spiritually. This wasn't just about temporary shelter or meals; it was about true transformation—a chance to grow closer to God, to heal, and to rebuild.

The chaplains welcomed me with open arms, and for the first time in a long while, I felt like I was exactly where I needed to be. I came to realize that **God had destined me to be there**. The missed buses, the setbacks—they weren't obstacles. They were part of God's redirection, leading me to this moment. I made the decision to stay, and in doing so, I embarked on a journey of self-reflection and spiritual growth that would change my life.

In that program, I began to flourish in my relationship with Jesus. It was a time of deep introspection—**one step at a time, I began the process of making amends for the wrongs I had committed**. I started to truly understand the depth of God's grace and how it extended even to someone like me, someone who had made so many mistakes. Each day, I felt a little more whole, a little more healed.

As I grew in my relationship with Christ, I knew there was a part of my past that I had to confront: **the wreckage I had caused in my marriage.** This was perhaps the hardest part. I had hurt my wife deeply, and while I had found salvation, I knew that I couldn't move forward without addressing the pain I had caused her.

I made several attempts to reach out to her—through social media, through phone calls—but each one went unanswered. **Silence.** It felt like confirmation that I had irreparably damaged our relationship, and the weight of that realization was crushing. But even in the face of that silence, I knew I needed closure. I couldn't undo the past, but I could at least make things right in the way I handled it going forward.

So I made a decision: I began saving money for a divorce. It wasn't what I wanted, but it seemed like the only way to close this chapter of my life and allow both of us to move on.

On the day I was supposed to go to the lawyer's office to pay for the divorce, **something unexpected happened**. As I walked toward the office, I felt an overwhelming sense of conviction. It wasn't just guilt or regret—it was the Holy Spirit stirring within me, prompting me to stop. I couldn't shake the feeling that I wasn't supposed to follow through with the divorce, at least not in this way. Instead, I felt God leading me to do something that, to my human mind, made no sense: **He was asking me to tithe the entire amount I had saved for the lawyer.**

This was an act of faith unlike anything I had ever done before. The money I had saved represented the only concrete step I had taken toward closure, and giving it up felt like giving up the last bit of control I had over the situation. But in obedience to God's prompting, I tithed the full amount, trusting that somehow, He had a plan.

And then, **three days later, the miracle happened**.

Out of the blue, my wife called me. I hadn't heard from her in what felt like an eternity, and now, she was reaching out. We began to talk, and in that conversation, I did something I had never fully done before: I apologized. **Not just a surface-level apology, but a heartfelt confession of everything I had done wrong.** I was specific about each offense. I admitted to the ways I had manipulated her, to the selfish decisions I had made to fulfill my own desires at her expense.

As I spoke, tears flowed on both sides. There was so much pain, so much hurt, but there was also something new—**a glimmer of hope, the possibility of healing**. The conversations that followed were filled with honesty, and while we didn't yet know where things would lead, we knew that God was working in both of our hearts.

During the second or third phone call, my wife asked me a question that cut straight to the heart: **"What brought about this change in you?"** It was a question I had been waiting for, one that opened the door to share the most important part of my journey—**the gospel**.

I told her about how my life had spiraled into darkness and how I had reached a point where I couldn't save myself. I shared how, in my lowest moment, I had cried out to Jesus and surrendered my life to Him. I explained that it wasn't by my own strength that I had changed, but by the transformative power of Christ's love and grace. With every word, I could feel the weight of the years of pain and separation lifting. **God was at work in that moment**, just as He had been from the very beginning.

Over the course of a few more phone calls, something miraculous happened. My wife, who had seen the worst of me, who had every reason to turn away, began to listen. The walls that had been built over years of hurt started to crumble, and in one of those conversations, she made the decision to accept Jesus as her Savior. **Through the phone, God reached into her heart**, just as He had done for me.

Within a month, we reconciled. But this time, we were not the same people we had been before. We had something we had never had before—**a marriage surrendered to Jesus.** The same God who had healed and restored me was now healing and restoring our marriage. It wasn't easy, and it wasn't immediate, but it was real. We began to pursue our newfound faith together, learning what it meant to walk in the light of Christ, not just as individuals but as a couple.

It is truly inspiring to reflect on how our marriage was transformed through **surrendering it under the authority of Jesus**. The love we once had was now something deeper, more profound—rooted not in our own strength, but in God's. We have faced many trials and hardships along the way, but this time we had something we never had before: a foundation built on Christ.

There were days when the past still tried to creep in, when the weight of our old wounds felt heavy. But each time, we returned to the truth that our marriage was no longer ours alone—it belonged to God. In those moments of struggle, we found ourselves relying on the strength of the Holy Spirit to guide us, to heal us, and to sustain us.

The lessons and truths contained in this book are glimpses of our own testimony and the profound revelations God has graciously bestowed upon us. They are not theoretical or abstract—they are born from the real, gritty journey of our lives, from the ashes of brokenness to the beauty of restoration. These truths have been **instrumental in shaping our marriage into what it is today**, guided by God's love and grace.

This is not just a story of two people finding their way back to each other; it's a testament to the transformative power of God's love. It's a story of **healing, redemption, and growth**—a story that reveals how Jesus can take what is broken and make it whole again. With Jesus at the center, we have experienced a profound change that has allowed us to navigate challenges and overcome obstacles that once seemed insurmountable.

We are deeply grateful for the blessings, wisdom, and the deepening of our faith that have accompanied our continued journey together. With every challenge we've faced, God has been there, leading us and refining us. As we embrace the lessons learned and the truths revealed to us, we feel compelled to share our story with others. **Our journey is not just for us**—it's for anyone who is seeking hope and restoration in their own marriages.

We believe that God can do for others what He has done for us. **May God continue to guide us, bless our marriage, and use our experiences to inspire and encourage others** on their own paths of faith and reconciliation. It is our prayer that this book will be a beacon of hope for those who feel lost or broken, and a reminder that with Christ, nothing is beyond repair.

One Flesh

Testimony Excerpt

When we entered into our marriage, we unknowingly built our foundation on the unstable sands of worldly wisdom. We thought we were deeply in love, and there was a certain truth to that—our love carried the excitement and novelty of youth. But it was not grounded in anything enduring. We knew the responsibilities that loomed ahead, especially with the anticipated arrival of our twin boys, but the weight of that responsibility was blurred by our lack of understanding of what true love, commitment, and faith really entailed.

Our love was, in many ways, like the parable of the seeds in Matthew 13:5-6. It had sprung up quickly, like seeds sown on rocky ground, but it lacked the deep roots needed to withstand the trials that were soon to come. We were navigating life together, but we were also two individuals still trying to find our way in a world that glorifies fleeting emotions, shallow desires, and personal ambition. The world taught us to chase after temporary happiness, neglecting the importance of a foundation built on something deeper, something eternal.

What we didn't realize at the time was that we had not anchored ourselves in the solid rock of God's truth. Our vision was clouded by the presence of sin, which subtly but surely seeped into our relationship, distorting our views of each other and of life. The sinful natures we harbored began to take control, particularly in my own life. Instead of turning to God, we sought external reasons to explain away the cracks in our relationship. For me, I blamed my own fractured family structure, marked by abuse and the absence of accountability. But no matter where we pointed the blame, the real issue was internal. Sin had taken root and grown, creating a breeding ground for distrust and disconnection between us.

The Apostle Paul speaks clearly about this in Romans 6:12-13: "Let not sin therefore reign in your mortal body, to make you obey its passions. Do not present your members to sin as instruments for unrighteousness." Yet, this is precisely what we were doing—presenting our lives and our marriage to the passions of the flesh instead of to the will of God.

These sins led us to make choices that would bring further turmoil. When we married during the late stages of our first pregnancy, it was a decision driven by the intensity of young love and a limited understanding of what it truly meant to be parents. We didn't yet grasp that being a father and a mother meant more than just providing materially for our children; it meant laying down a foundation of spiritual leadership, which we were ill-equipped to provide at the time.

Those early years were hard. Our marriage was filled with tension, dishonesty, and unmet expectations. Rather than working together as one, we were two separate people, operating under conflicting ideologies. We had yet to learn what Jesus taught in Mark 10:8: "and the two shall become one flesh. So they are no longer two but one flesh." We were far from this kind of unity.

Our interactions with one another were reactive, driven by emotion rather than reflection or humility, which only deepened the divide. But even in these dark moments, God was at work. The hardships we faced—though painful—were not without purpose. Like clay in the potter's hands, our marriage was being shaped, refined, and strengthened, even though at the time, we couldn't see it.

What is one flesh?

In marriage and throughout Scripture, the concept of becoming "one flesh" is often referenced. It is a profound statement, typically declared by ministers during marriage ceremonies, signifying the deep, spiritual union between husband and wife. This term finds its origins in the book of Genesis, particularly in chapter 2, verses 23 and 24, where it says:

> *"Then the man said, 'This is now bone of my bones, and flesh of my flesh; she shall be called 'woman,' for she was taken out of man.' For this reason, a man shall leave his father and mother and be united to his wife, and they will become one flesh."* (Genesis 2:23-24, NASB)

To fully appreciate the weight of these verses, it's essential to examine the context in which this declaration is made. Prior to this moment, God had created the entire universe—He spoke the heavens, the earth, and all life into existence with a word. And at the pinnacle of creation, God formed man from the dust of the earth and breathed life into him, creating Adam. He placed Adam in the Garden of Eden with the responsibility to work it and take care of it (Genesis 2:15). But God saw that it was not good for Adam to be alone, and in His wisdom, He determined to create a companion, a helper suited for him.

The term "helper" is significant because it reflects the intentionality behind God's design. When God speaks of providing Adam a helper, it is not in the sense of someone who is subordinate or inferior. Rather, this helper was to be a counterpart, a partner who complements Adam in every way, physically, emotionally, and spiritually. God was not just filling a void in Adam's life but establishing a divine standard for companionship and unity in marriage.

Before creating this suitable helper, God brought forth the animals from the field and the birds of the sky for Adam to name. Adam evaluated each creature, but none of them met the divine standard of partnership that God intended. This demonstrates the uniqueness of humanity—no animal could fulfill the role of an equal, complementary partner to Adam.

And so, in a miraculous act of creation, God caused Adam to fall into a deep sleep, took one of his ribs, and fashioned the woman from it (Genesis 2:21-22). The symbolism here is profound. Eve was not created from Adam's head to rule over him, nor from his feet to be trampled by him, but from his side, close to his heart, to be his equal, his partner, his helpmate. This act not only emphasizes the unity between man and woman but also underscores the intimacy and interconnectedness that God designed marriage to reflect.

When Adam saw Eve, his response was one of awe and recognition. "Bone of my bones and flesh of my flesh" signifies that Adam saw in Eve a reflection of himself—someone who was like him, yet distinct. It's this recognition of shared identity, purpose, and value that underpins the biblical concept of marriage. The phrase "one flesh" speaks to a unity that is far deeper than mere physical closeness. It represents a fusion of lives, hearts, and purposes, where husband and wife are no longer two, but one. This unity is meant to mirror the oneness found within the Godhead itself, as Jesus later emphasized in Matthew 19:6 when He said, "So they are no longer two, but one flesh. Therefore what God has joined together, let no one separate."

This divine design for marriage reveals that the unity between man and woman is not merely for companionship but is also a reflection of God's covenantal relationship with humanity. As Paul writes in Ephesians 5:31-32, this "one flesh" union is a mystery that points to Christ and the church. Just as a husband and wife become one, Christ and His church are united through the bond of His sacrifice and love. This covenantal aspect of marriage calls us to see marriage not just as a contract between two people but as a holy institution established by God.

For Adam and Eve, this unity was perfect at the moment of their creation. However, sin would soon enter the picture, distorting and marring this beautiful design. But even in its brokenness, God's standard for marriage remains a reflection of His enduring covenant with us, a covenant grounded in love, sacrifice, and unity.

The institution of marriage is designed to reflect the profound unity and mutual completion that God intended between man and woman. When a man discovers the partner whom God has ordained for him, and they enter into the sacred covenant of marriage, they become one flesh—a mystery that surpasses the physical union alone. This union stretches into every aspect of their being: emotionally, spiritually, and relationally. No longer are they two separate individuals. Instead, they are joined in such a way that they now exist as a unified whole, intricately woven together by God Himself.

Understanding this concept of becoming "one flesh" allows us to grasp the true purpose and intricate design of marriage. Marriage is not just a social contract or a partnership of convenience—it is a divine covenant, a holy union. In this union, God brings together two individuals, each uniquely created, to form a harmonious partnership that reflects His love and creative intent. As Genesis 2:24 illustrates, "a man shall leave his father and his mother and be joined to his wife, and they shall become one flesh." This joining is not merely symbolic; it is a spiritual reality where the husband and wife complement and support one another, filling in the gaps and inadequacies that each may have experienced individually.

In Ephesians 5:25-28, Paul describes the sacrificial love that a husband is to have for his wife, likening it to Christ's love for the church. He writes, "Husbands, love your wives, just as Christ loved the church and gave Himself up for her to make her holy... In this same way, husbands ought to love their wives as their own bodies. He who loves his wife loves himself." Here, Paul highlights the depth of responsibility and care that is inherent in the marriage relationship. Just as Christ gave His life to sanctify the church, so too are husbands called to lay down their own interests for the sake of their wives, demonstrating a selfless love that mirrors Christ's.

The concept of "one flesh" carries with it this profound sense of responsibility and care, much like the way we instinctively protect and nurture the members of our own body. When a man loves his wife, he is loving himself, as she is now an inseparable part of him. This responsibility is more than just providing for physical needs; it involves spiritual protection, emotional support, and mutual growth in their walk with God. Just as a body works in unison to ensure its health and well-being, so too should a husband and wife work together in harmony, ensuring that both are growing in their love for God and one another.

An analogy that captures the essence of this oneness is the act of using an oven mitt to remove a hot pan from the oven. When a finger accidentally touches the scorching pan, our immediate and instinctive response is to pull away in order to prevent injury. This reaction occurs without conscious thought, driven by the innate drive to protect and care for our body. In the same way, within the context of marriage, a husband and wife are called to instinctively care for and protect one another. The pains or struggles of one should automatically trigger a response from the other, not out of duty, but out of love, because they are now one flesh. Just as we would not allow harm to come to our own body without reacting, so too should we guard and protect our spouse with the same instinctive concern.

In this oneness, the couple becomes a living example of the divine relationship God desires with His people. Just as He cares for us—tenderly, sacrificially, and relentlessly—we too are called to care for our spouses with that same depth of commitment and devotion. The marriage relationship thus becomes a reflection of God's covenant with humanity:

steadfast, enduring, and marked by an unbreakable bond of love and responsibility.

In the sacred bond of marriage, our spouse becomes an extension of ourselves—our own flesh and member. Just as we naturally act in the best interest of our physical body, we are called to act in the best interest of our spouse. The apostle Paul addresses this profound truth in Ephesians 5:29-31, where he emphasizes the nourishing and cherishing of our own flesh, drawing a parallel to the way Christ cares for His Church. Paul's words echo the divine design for marriage, revealing that just as Christ nurtures His body, the Church, so too should husbands and wives care for one another as parts of a single, unified whole.

Ephesians 5:29-31 (NASB) states:
"For no one ever hated his own flesh, but nourishes and cherishes it, just as Christ also does the church, because we are parts of His body. FOR THIS REASON A MAN SHALL LEAVE HIS FATHER AND MOTHER AND BE JOINED TO HIS WIFE, AND THE TWO SHALL BECOME ONE FLESH."

This passage reinforces that the bond between a husband and wife is not only physical, but it extends into the emotional, spiritual, and relational aspects of life. Paul's teaching reveals that the love and care we provide for our spouse mirrors the love Christ has for His Church. He does not care for us intermittently or only in times of crisis. Instead, He is our constant source of strength, provision, and guidance. Similarly, our care for our spouse must not be confined to significant decisions or grand gestures, but it should be displayed in the seemingly small, everyday moments of life.

Loving and honoring our spouse means being attentive to their needs, responding with genuine care, and going above and beyond when necessary. This extends to the daily acts of kindness, the thoughtful words, and the quiet moments where we choose to prioritize their well-being over our own. It is about serving them with the same selflessness with which we would protect and nourish our own body.

In many ways, this is a reflection of Philippians 2:3-4, which says, *"Do nothing out of selfish ambition or vain conceit. Rather, in humility value others above yourselves, not looking to your own interests but each of you to the interests of the others."* Within marriage, this humble, Christ-like mindset should be at the heart of every interaction. In choosing to value our spouse's needs, desires, and well-being above our own, we fulfill God's call to love them as we love ourselves.

It's easy to focus on the larger, more noticeable aspects of marriage—major decisions, career changes, or the big celebrations. However, God calls us to a deeper understanding of what it means to be "one flesh." It is in the day-to-day, in the mundane tasks, that our love for our spouse is truly tested and refined. It's in listening when they speak, responding to their needs with kindness, and choosing patience and grace over frustration and selfishness.

By actively expressing love and honoring our spouse, we ultimately honor God. The love we pour into our marriage is a reflection of our love and obedience to Him. As Christ loved the Church and gave Himself up for her, so we too are called to live sacrificially within our marriages, cherishing and nurturing our spouse as a vital part of our own body.

The beauty of this covenant is that it mirrors the relationship God desires with us—a relationship built on sacrificial love, unity, and devotion. In marriage, we are given the sacred privilege of reflecting this divine relationship. When we care for our spouse in the small, often unnoticed ways, we are not only strengthening the bond of our marriage, but we are also participating in God's grand design for His people. In doing so, we display His love to the world through our union.

Ephesians 5:28 further emphasizes the profound significance of husbands loving their wives as they love their own bodies. Paul writes, *"So husbands also ought to love their own wives as their own bodies. He who loves his own wife loves himself."* This verse underscores a vital principle of marriage: the mutual interdependence and unity that God intended, where the well-being and nurturing of our spouse are intricately connected to our own well-being.

The concept of "one flesh" teaches us that our lives are no longer separate from those of our spouse; instead, they are deeply intertwined. This interconnection means that our spouse's happiness, fulfillment, and growth directly impact our own. When we love and care for our spouse wholeheartedly, we are, in effect, loving and caring for ourselves. This truth calls us to a level of commitment that goes beyond convenience—it requires genuine selflessness and sacrificial love.

The love that Paul speaks of in Ephesians is not merely a feeling; it is an intentional act of the will. It is the kind of love that mirrors Christ's love for us—steadfast, enduring, and willing to lay down personal desires for the good of the other. Christ gave Himself up for the Church, not because it was easy or convenient, but because it was necessary for our redemption and ultimate flourishing. In the same way, we are called to give of ourselves for the sake of our spouse, putting their needs before our own.

In practical terms, this means striving to cultivate a marriage built on humility and a genuine desire to see our spouse flourish. It is about choosing to serve even when we feel tired, to listen even when we are distracted, and to encourage even when we are burdened. These acts of love may seem small, but they form the foundation of a thriving marriage. As we prioritize our spouse's well-being, we create an environment in which they can grow, find fulfillment, and experience the fullness of God's design for their life.

This kind of sacrificial love is beautifully depicted in 1 Corinthians 13:4-7, where Paul describes love as patient, kind, not envious or boastful, and always protecting, trusting, hoping, and persevering. Within the context of marriage, these attributes become the building blocks for a deep, lasting bond. When we love our spouse in this way, we reflect God's heart for us, and our marriage becomes a testament to the love of Christ.

By embracing the concept of being "one flesh," we acknowledge that our lives are not just linked but intricately bound together by God's design. Their successes and joys are ours to celebrate, and their struggles and pains are ours to share. In this way, we become not only partners in life but also reflections of the unity that God desires with His people—a unity marked by love, faithfulness, and unwavering commitment.

When we live out this truth in our marriage, we do more than just nurture a strong marital bond—we honor the divine design that God has established. We honor the covenant that we entered before God and others. And most importantly, we honor God Himself, who has given us the sacred privilege of experiencing and reflecting His love through the union of marriage.

In this journey of loving sacrificially and living as "one flesh," we come to understand that marriage is ultimately about glorifying God. It is a relationship that refines us, teaches us, and draws us closer to Him. As we love our spouse with the same depth and devotion with which Christ loves us, we become instruments of His grace, reflecting His character in a world in desperate need of true, godly love.

Personal pursuit of Jesus

Testimony excerpt

After both of us experienced the life-changing power of salvation, we came to a profound realization: Jesus was more important than anything else in our lives. We understood that, for our marriage to thrive, Christ had to be at the center. This revelation brought a newfound hope and clarity to our relationship. However, we quickly learned that even after being reconciled under God, the world's influence could subtly creep back into our lives and marriage. The sanctification process, though transformative, doesn't eliminate past wounds or struggles overnight. We found ourselves navigating through uncharted territory, feeling as though we were starting over, trying to figure everything out for the first time.

The wounds from our past, the scars of brokenness, still had a way of resurfacing, bringing pain into moments that we thought were healed. These old hurts, whether from childhood or from the mistakes we had made earlier in our marriage, sometimes felt like weights we couldn't fully shake off. It was in these moments that we realized healing is not always immediate; it's a process that requires time, grace, and, most importantly, surrender to God. As Romans 12:2 reminds us, we needed to be transformed by the renewing of our minds, not conforming to the patterns of this world.

Yet, even as believers, we found ourselves vulnerable to the snares of the flesh. Temptation didn't disappear once we gave our lives to Christ. We were still susceptible to the very sins we thought we had left behind—lustful desires, worldly distractions, and selfish ambitions. These struggles often manifested in how we communicated, or rather, how we failed to communicate. The strain from our individual battles spilled over into our marriage, creating distance where there should have been unity. We were like soldiers fighting separate wars, each isolated and entrenched in our own struggles, when what we really needed was to fight together, side by side, under the banner of Christ.

There were days when the weight of it all felt unbearable. The idea of separation, though something we desperately wanted to avoid, loomed over us like a dark cloud. There were moments when we felt as though we were on the verge of giving up again, exhausted by the constant battle between our flesh and our spirit. We knew deep down that something had to change—that our current way of doing things wasn't sustainable. Ephesians 6:12 reminded us that our battle wasn't against flesh and blood but against spiritual forces that sought to destroy the very fabric of our marriage.

In our search for healing and restoration, we decided to seek counsel from the elders in our church. Through their wisdom and guidance, we began to gain a clearer understanding of what it truly meant to build a marriage centered on Christ. They offered us biblical principles that we had overlooked or misunderstood in our previous efforts to fix things on our own. Proverbs 15:22 says, "Plans fail for lack of counsel, but with many advisers they succeed." Seeking the wisdom of others was one of the most humbling and necessary steps we took on our path toward a healthier marriage.

During these conversations, we learned the importance of not just praying together as a couple but also pursuing Jesus individually. It became clear to us that our personal relationship with Christ was the foundation upon which a strong marriage is built. Without cultivating that intimate, individual relationship with Jesus, we were attempting to pour from empty cups. We realized that personal spiritual growth wasn't just about our own walk with God, but it was directly tied to the health and vitality of our marriage. As we each grew closer to Christ, the fruits of that growth—love, patience, humility, and kindness—began to overflow into our marriage.

The elders also introduced us to practical ways to implement these truths in our daily lives. They encouraged us to make time for regular devotionals, both together and separately, and to intentionally speak life into each other. We started to practice forgiveness in small ways, recognizing that unresolved bitterness had been a silent enemy in our home. We began to communicate more openly about our struggles, not out of accusation, but with a spirit of grace and understanding, remembering that we were both works in progress under the hand of God.

In this chapter of our journey, we focused on the concept of personal pursuit of Jesus and its application within our marriage. It wasn't enough to rely on each other to fill the voids that only God could fill. We learned that by prioritizing our individual relationship with Christ, we were better equipped to love each other as Christ loved us. John 15:5 says, "I am the vine, you are the branches. If you remain in me and I in you, you will bear much fruit; apart from me you can do nothing." This verse became a cornerstone of our journey. We understood that without abiding in Christ, our efforts would be fruitless.

As we pursued personal growth in Christ, we found that our marriage became stronger, more resilient, and more grace-filled. The transformative power of Jesus began to heal not just our individual wounds, but the cracks in our relationship as well. By making Him our focus, we were able to cultivate a marriage that honored God and reflected His love to the world.

Personal pursuit of Jesus

It is indeed a common notion to perceive marriage as a fifty-fifty partnership, where each spouse contributes equally to meet the needs of the relationship. However, this perspective may be flawed and potentially problematic. Relying solely on each partner's half-share can create difficulties, particularly when one individual is unable to fulfill their expected fifty percent due to personal challenges or circumstances.

A healthier approach to marriage involves viewing it as a commitment to give one hundred percent on the part of both spouses. Each person commits to contributing their entire being and all they have to offer. In this mindset, there is no fixed expectation of a specific division or balance. Instead, the focus is on wholeheartedly investing oneself in marriage. This kind of love echoes the selfless, sacrificial love that Christ has for the Church. As described in Ephesians 5:25, "Husbands, love your wives, just as Christ loved the church and gave himself up for her." The model of Christ's love is one of total commitment, of giving one's all even when the other party may not be able to fully reciprocate.

Inevitably, there will be seasons in life when one spouse may face personal struggles or limitations that prevent them from giving their full one hundred percent. However, in a marriage built on the foundation of mutual commitment, these shortcomings can be addressed and overcome. The missing percentage is not a cause for blame or judgment but rather an opportunity to come together as a couple, lay those challenges at the foot of the cross, and support and pray for one another. Galatians 6:2 reminds us to "carry each other's burdens, and in this way, you will fulfill the law of Christ." When one spouse is weak, the other has the privilege and duty to help carry that burden, reflecting Christ's love in action.

Furthermore, the biblical principle of covenant is foundational to understanding this full investment in marriage. Unlike a contract, which is often based on equal exchange and can be broken if terms are not met, a covenant is an unbreakable promise. In Malachi 2:14, marriage is referred to as a covenant before God, and this emphasizes the solemnity and enduring nature of the commitment. Viewing marriage as a covenant helps each spouse to see their role not as conditional upon the other's actions, but as an unchanging promise to love, honor, and support no matter the circumstances.

Jesus Himself demonstrated this kind of covenant love through His relationship with humanity. He gave everything for us, even when we were unable to give anything in return (Romans 5:8). In marriage, this principle can be seen when spouses choose to love and serve each other even in times of weakness or difficulty, imitating the unconditional love of Christ. It is through this sacrificial love that marriages can not only survive but thrive, growing stronger in the face of challenges.

Marriage, then, is less about keeping score and more about pouring oneself out in love, just as Christ did for us. It is about seeking unity and wholeness as two become one flesh (Genesis 2:24). When both spouses embrace this one-hundred-percent mindset, they are better equipped to weather the storms of life, leaning on God's strength and grace. As Ecclesiastes 4:12 reminds us, "Though one may be overpowered, two can defend themselves. A cord of three strands is not quickly broken." In a marriage where both spouses give their all, and where God is at the center, there is an unbreakable strength that can withstand any trial.

By approaching marriage with an attitude of giving our all, we create a safe space where grace, understanding, and support can flourish. It allows for the recognition that challenges will arise, and it is in these moments that the true strength and resilience of the marriage are revealed. Through unconditional love, mutual understanding, and shared faith, couples can navigate the ebb and flow of life's seasons, ensuring that the foundation of their commitment remains steadfast.

To articulate the essence of a Christ-centered marriage is to recognize the transformative power it can bring to the relationship. By seeking fulfillment in Jesus rather than relying solely on our spouse, we open ourselves to a deeper understanding of grace and the ability to extend it to one another. This perspective allows us to cover our spouse's shortcomings with mercy and grace, knowing that our ultimate fulfillment comes from our relationship with God. As Philippians 4:19 states, "And my God will meet all your needs according to the riches of his glory in Christ Jesus." This reminds us that our needs are met by God, freeing us from placing unrealistic expectations on our spouse.

In a Christ-centered marriage, disagreements and arguments are approached differently. Rather than striving to win or prove a point, the focus shifts to seeking guidance and resolution through prayer. By pausing to pray and lay our concerns and issues at the foot of Jesus, we invite His wisdom, peace, and reconciliation into the situation. James 1:5 encourages us, "If any of you lacks wisdom, you should ask God, who gives generously to all without finding fault, and it will be given to you." This practice acknowledges that true fulfillment and direction come from God, rather than relying solely on each other for worldly satisfaction. By seeking God's wisdom, couples can move forward in unity, fostering an environment where love, respect, and mutual understanding prevail, ultimately strengthening the marriage bond.

To cultivate a healthy and Christ-centered marriage, it is crucial for both spouses to agree and commit to seeking and loving God above all else in their lives. By shifting the focus away from our spouse's performance or shortcomings, and instead relentlessly pursuing a personal relationship with Christ, we create an environment of grace, understanding, and growth. It is important to prioritize individual time with God alongside shared spiritual practices as a couple. Matthew 6:33 emphasizes, "But seek first his kingdom and his righteousness, and all these things will be given to you as well." By placing God first, both individually and collectively, the marriage is strengthened.

By individually pursuing God and fostering a deep connection with Him, we become better equipped to support and pray for our spouse in times of failure or struggle. This approach strengthens the bond between husband and wife, fostering a deeper level of love, support, and reliance on God's grace within the marriage. As Colossians 3:13 encourages, "Bear with each other and forgive one another if any of you has a grievance against someone. Forgive as the Lord forgave you." This spirit of forgiveness and grace is cultivated through a personal walk with God, allowing each spouse to extend the same to their partner.

In essence, a Christ-centered marriage is one in which both spouses continuously seek God's guidance and fulfillment, understanding that true satisfaction and direction come from Him alone. By embracing this mindset, the wife is no longer seeking the fulfillment of her heart from her husband but from God, and likewise, the husband from his wife. If our need for fulfillment and strength comes from the Lord and not our spouse, we are able to aid and support our spouse in their hardships rather than ridicule them for their shortcomings. Proverbs 3:5-6 reminds us, "Trust in the Lord with all your heart and lean not on your own understanding; in all your ways submit to him, and he will make your paths straight." By trusting in God rather than leaning on our own limited understanding or expecting our spouse to be our ultimate source of strength, we cultivate a marriage that is rooted in God's grace and capable of enduring any challenge.

      Allow me to provide a practical and meaningful approach to nurturing your faith and relationship with God within the busyness of life, because finding dedicated time for Bible studies as a couple may be challenging. By individually pursuing your own paths to Jesus and then sharing your experiences and insights with one another during relaxed moments, such as meals or downtime, you create opportunities for spiritual growth and connection, while not requiring a scheduled time of fellowship. Hebrews 4:12 reminds us of the power of God's Word to penetrate deep within us, discerning our thoughts and intentions. As you both individually seek God, your hearts are laid bare before Him, allowing His Word to shape and guide your lives. When you come together, this shared pursuit of Jesus leads to a deeper love, increased grace, and a greater capacity to extend mercy to one another. This understanding is vital in maintaining a strong Christian marriage, as it reinforces the truth that your fulfillment and needs are ultimately found in God, not solely in each other.

Hebrews 4:12 (NASB) states, "For the word of God is living and active, and sharper than any two-edged sword, even penetrating as far as the division of soul and spirit, of both joints and marrow, and able to judge the thoughts and intentions of the heart." In this personal pursuit of Jesus, it is important to recognize the distinction between happiness and joy. While happiness is often temporary and dependent on external circumstances, joy is a deep-rooted sense of contentment and gladness that transcends hardship. By focusing on joy rather than chasing fleeting happiness, you and your spouse can navigate challenges and trials with a steadfast faith. Difficult times can even yield beautiful growth and transformation if you remain anchored in your faith and trust in God's plan. James 1:2-3 encourages us, "Consider it pure joy, my brothers and sisters, whenever you face trials of many kinds, because you know that the testing of your faith produces perseverance." By embracing joy through faith, couples can find strength and purpose in the midst of trials, ultimately growing closer to each other and to God.

By meeting each other in your individual journeys, extending grace and mercy, and remaining steadfast in faith, you create a solid foundation for a Christ-centered relationship. May you continue to grow together, supporting one another, and experiencing the joy that comes from walking closely with Jesus.

Romans 5:1-5 (NASB) states, "Therefore, having been justified by faith, we have peace with God through our Lord Jesus Christ, through whom we also have obtained our introduction by faith into this grace in which we stand; and we celebrate in hope of the glory of God. And not only this, but we also celebrate in our tribulations, knowing that tribulation brings about perseverance; and perseverance, proven character; and proven character, hope; and hope does not disappoint, because the love of God has been poured out within our hearts through the Holy Spirit who was given to us." When we personally pursue Jesus and experience His peace and joy, we are equipped to extend even greater mercy and grace to our spouse. As we encounter challenges and difficult seasons in life, we can hold onto the hope that lies on the other side, knowing that God is faithful and will lead us to the mountain peak.

In 1 Peter chapter 1, the apostle Peter speaks about the living hope we have through the resurrection of Jesus Christ. He encourages believers to rejoice, even amid trials, knowing that our faith is being refined and tested for a purpose. Peter emphasizes the enduring nature of our inheritance in heaven and the joy that awaits us. This perspective helps us find peace and hope in God's plan, even when our hearts may be hurting in the valleys of life.

By anchoring ourselves in the truth of God's promises and the hope of eternal life, we can navigate the challenges of marriage with a sense of peace and assurance. This allows us to extend mercy and grace to our spouse, understanding that they too may be going through their own valleys and need our support and understanding. Ultimately, the personal pursuit of Jesus not only strengthens our individual relationship with Him but also enriches our marriage. As we rely on God's peace and joy, we are better able to walk alongside our spouse, offering them the same mercy, grace, and understanding that God extends to us.

In summary, this chapter has emphasized the importance of a Christ-centered approach to marriage, where both spouses give one hundred percent of themselves, mirroring the sacrificial love of Christ. It has explored the concept of marriage as a covenant, the need to seek fulfillment in God rather than each other, and the power of prayer and shared faith in resolving conflicts. The importance of personal spiritual growth and its impact on the marital relationship has been highlighted, encouraging couples to support and uplift one another, especially during challenging times. By anchoring in God's promises, embracing joy through faith, and cultivating an environment of grace, couples can navigate the valleys of life with hope, ultimately building a marriage that is strong, enduring, and reflective of God's love.

May the truths shared in 1 Peter chapter 1 continue to inspire and encourage you in your personal pursuit of Jesus and in building a strong, Christ-centered marriage.

1 Peter 1:6-9 (NASB) states, "In this you greatly rejoice, even though now for a little while, if necessary, you have been distressed by various trials, so that the proof of your faith, being more precious than gold which perishes though tested by fire, may be found to result in praise, glory, and honor at the revelation of Jesus Christ; and though you have not seen Him, you love Him, and though you do not see Him now, but believe in Him, you greatly rejoice with joy inexpressible and full of glory, obtaining as the outcome of your faith, the salvation of your souls."

Live in Truth

Testimony Excerpt

Throughout our marriage, even after finding salvation in Christ, we faced moments of weakness and hidden struggles. One such struggle was my addiction to pornography, which I desperately tried to conceal from my wife. Deep down, I sensed the conviction of the Holy Spirit, knowing that my actions were wrong and feeling ashamed of the darkness that sometimes consumed my heart. Unfortunately, instead of confronting my addiction honestly, I chose to engage in deceit, weaving a web of lies to shield my shortcomings, unknowingly causing a rift in the intimate connection we were meant to share.

My wife, with her keen intuition, always had a sense that something was amiss, as if she possessed the abilities of Spiderwoman herself. Yet, I stubbornly clung to my fabricated falsehoods, foolishly hoping that time alone would dissolve the pain and mend the damage caused by my lies. However, much like feeding a stray dog, my actions only perpetuated the cycle, prolonging the agony we both experienced.

But the transformation and healing in this area of our marriage did not come without sacrifice and difficult lessons from our Heavenly Father. It was only when I truly surrendered my struggle to the Lord, choosing vulnerability over pride, that things began to change. James 5:16 tells us, "Therefore confess your sins to each other and pray for each other so that you may be healed." This verse became pivotal for me, as I recognized the power of confession and the importance of inviting God into the darkest corners of my heart. By opening up to my wife and seeking her forgiveness, I began to break free from the chains of secrecy that had held me captive for so long.

Through dedicated prayer and earnest study of Scripture, I reached several profound conclusions that have shaped our understanding of intimacy and its sacred significance. One of those revelations was that intimacy in marriage is not just a physical connection but also a spiritual covenant designed by God. Ephesians 5:31-32 speaks of the mystery of marriage, comparing it to the relationship between Christ and the Church. I came to understand that my addiction was not only harming my wife but also dishonoring the sacred bond that God intended for us. True intimacy is built on trust, transparency, and mutual respect—qualities that reflect Christ's love for His Church.

I also realized that, in my attempts to satisfy my own desires, I was missing the deeper fulfillment that God had designed for marriage. Proverbs 5:18-19 encourages husbands to rejoice in the wife of their youth, to find delight in the spouse God has given them. When I began to see intimacy not as a means to fulfill my own selfish needs but as an opportunity to honor my wife and glorify God, our relationship began to heal. I learned to seek God first, trusting that He would restore what had been broken and bring true joy to our marriage.

Moreover, I have learned where and how to encounter God in the midst of our intimate connection, discovering that true fulfillment and transformation can be found when we align our hearts with His divine purpose. Intimacy became an act of worship, a way to honor the covenant we made before God. As we prayed together and invited God into every aspect of our marriage, including our physical relationship, we experienced a depth of connection that we had never known before. Hebrews 13:4 reminds us that marriage should be honored by all, and the marriage bed kept pure. This became our goal—to honor God through our intimacy, keeping it pure and sacred.

It is through these struggles and the lessons learned that our marriage has been refined, deepening our understanding of the sanctity of intimacy and guiding us towards a path of restoration and growth. We learned that God's grace is sufficient, even in our weakness (2 Corinthians 12:9). The journey was not easy, and it required both of us to extend forgiveness and grace, just as Christ has forgiven us. Yet, through the power of God, what was once broken has been made whole, and our marriage stands as a testimony to His redeeming love.

May the revelations shared in this chapter serve as a beacon of hope and wisdom for others who may be facing similar challenges in their own relationships. God is able to heal and restore, and when we allow Him into our brokenness, He creates beauty from the ashes. Let this be an encouragement to those struggling in silence—God's love is greater than our darkest secrets, and His desire is to bring us into the light of true intimacy and freedom.

Live in Truth

The Scriptures provide us with profound insights into the character of God and the nature of our relationship with Him. In this section, aptly titled "Live in Truth," we aim to emphasize the paramount importance of living in truth with God and, consequently, cultivating a foundation of truth within our marriages. Jesus Himself instructs us to worship in spirit and in truth, highlighting the essentiality of embracing truth in our relationship with God.

John 4:24 (NASB) "God is spirit, and those who worship Him must worship in spirit and truth."

In the first chapter of this book, we explored the concept of "one flesh" and its connection to Jesus' comparison between His relationship with the Church and the sacred union between a man and a woman in marriage. Jesus, being the ultimate teacher and often referred to as Rabbi, serves as our ultimate example. Through the guidance and work of the Holy Spirit, we can embark on a transformative journey of learning and growth, progressively becoming more like Him. This ongoing process, known as progressive sanctification, allows us to develop a resemblance to His character, ultimately bestowing His abundant grace and mercy upon our lives and the lives of those destined to share our journey.

Therefore, as we observe the character of Christ, let us delve into a few additional verses in the book of Ephesians, which further illuminate the transformative power of His character in our lives and relationships. These verses serve as guiding lights, directing us towards a path of truth, unity, and profound love within the sacred covenant of marriage.

Ephesians 4:2-3 encourages us to "be completely humble and gentle; be patient, bearing with one another in love. Make every effort to keep the unity of the Spirit through the bond of peace." These qualities are crucial for maintaining harmony in marriage. Humility and gentleness allow us to put our spouse's needs before our own, while patience and love help us endure challenges together. When we commit to keeping the unity of the Spirit, we invite God's presence into our marriage, fostering a bond that cannot easily be broken.

Furthermore, Ephesians 4:25 urges us to "put off falsehood and speak truthfully to your neighbor." In the context of marriage, our spouse is our closest neighbor, and living in truth means being open and honest with one another. Lies and deceit create division, but truth brings freedom and unity. By embracing honesty, even when it is difficult, we honor God and our spouse, creating a safe environment where love can flourish.

Ephesians 5:21 also teaches us to "submit to one another out of reverence for Christ." Submission in marriage is not about control or dominance but about mutual respect and service. When both partners submit to one another, they reflect the love of Christ, who gave Himself up for the Church. This kind of submission fosters an atmosphere of trust and security, where both partners feel valued and cherished.

Ephesians 5:25-27 (NASB) "25 Husbands, love your wives, just as Christ also loved the church and gave Himself up for her, 26 so that He might sanctify her, having cleansed her by the washing of water with the word, 27 that He might present to Himself the church in all her glory, having no spot or wrinkle or any such thing; but that she would be holy and blameless."

The powerful words of Ephesians 5 resound with the depth of Jesus' love for us, as well as the profound responsibility placed upon husbands. Just as Christ loved the Church and selflessly gave Himself up for her, husbands are called to emulate this sacrificial love for their wives. Through such love, husbands become instrumental in the sanctification of their wives, cleansing them through the transformative power of the Word. The goal is for the wives to stand before their husbands and God, radiating in glory, without a spot or wrinkle, but holy and blameless.

Witnessing Jesus' instructions on how we should treat our wives and the kind of love we should extend to them, we are now able to add more pieces to the puzzle of a Christ-centered marriage. As we strive to become more like Christ, it is crucial to understand the means by which we can achieve this remarkable feat. A scripture that has personally resonated with me in this regard is found in 1 John 1:7. This verse illuminates the concept of walking in the light, which is a characteristic of God Himself. Light and darkness have no fellowship with each other; they are fundamentally incompatible. This truth should profoundly shape our decision-making process.

1 John 1:7 (NASB) "but if we walk in the Light as He Himself is in the Light, we have fellowship with one another, and the blood of Jesus His Son cleanses us from all sin."

God invites us to walk in the light, just as He is in the light, and promises fellowship with Him as a result. To cultivate a closer relationship with the Creator, I must purposefully and intentionally seek to live as He does. By doing so, the blood of Jesus cleanses us from our sins, setting us free from their grip. God, who sees and judges the hearts of individuals, understands the destructive nature of porn in the lives of men. Therefore, in my pursuit of Christ, I strive to live a life that seeks His presence. In order to dwell in His light, I must walk according to the guidance of the Holy Spirit, and this can only be accomplished by embracing and living in truth.

Hence, as we wholeheartedly pursue Christ in our personal lives and within our marriages, walking in the light of His truth, we experience the transformative power of His love, grace, and sanctification. It is in this journey that we can truly reflect His character and embrace the profound depths of intimacy, unity, and holiness within the sacred covenant of marriage.

In the context of marriage, truth holds immeasurable significance. When we attempt to live outside the boundaries of truth, we not only deceive our spouses but also deprive ourselves of the joy and fulfillment of our covenant before God. The moment we choose to hide something from our spouse, particularly something sinful, we step out of the light and fellowship with God is disrupted. The conviction of the Holy Spirit makes sure we are aware of this misalignment. In my own experience, when I engaged in such behavior, not only did I conceal the truth, but I also had to bear the weight of shame that accompanied it. One truly comprehends the depth of shame when their heart is exposed before God, and their sin is laid bare.

This shame gives birth to a profound and persistent pain that serves as a constant reminder of our transgressions and shortcomings. Its presence erects barriers that hinder the development of an intimate relationship, both with God and with our spouse. One may believe that they can hide their actions well enough to preserve their marriage, but the truth remains: it is impossible to do so. When we hide our sins or maintain a facade of falsehood, we must also safeguard our vulnerability, lest our deceit be discovered. Vulnerability is the key to fostering an intimate and authentic love with Jesus and our spouse. It is through vulnerability that we are able to approach the altar, pouring out our hearts before God, fully aware that He sees us as we truly are—He discerns our deepest thoughts and knows our innermost being. In His infinite love and boundless forgiveness, He accepts us.

Embracing truth and vulnerability not only restores our relationship with God but also paves the way for the restoration of intimacy within our marriages. It is through transparent honesty and the recognition of our imperfections that we create an environment conducive to healing and growth. The power of vulnerability lies in its ability to cultivate trust, open communication, and a deeper sense of connection. By acknowledging our weaknesses and seeking forgiveness, we invite God's grace and mercy to transform our hearts and restore the sacred bond of love within our marriages. In this journey of truth and vulnerability, we can experience the profound joy of being fully known and fully loved by both God and our spouse.

We should also express that vulnerability to our spouse, for they are our intimate partner, chosen by God to be united with us as one flesh in His image of love and sacrifice, mirroring Christ's relationship with the church. When we reach this place of openness and authenticity, the burden of guilt and shame that once weighed heavily upon our spirits will be lifted. We can love and serve our spouse in truth, free from the hindrance that sin once brought into our lives.

Therefore, just as Christ lived for the church, embodying the characteristics of God, we too are called to live for our wives. We are called to walk in truth with them, sharing our hurts and struggles honestly. Although it may cause initial pain, I assure you that your spouse would prefer to know the truth so that she can pray for you and stand alongside you in support. Similarly, pray together, humbling yourselves at the foot of the cross, and allow the Holy Spirit and the Word of God to guide your hearts, empowering you to resist sin. Continually seek God by walking in the light, just as He is in the light, and if you stumble once again, remember that God examines the depths of our hearts. Through our sincere pursuit of Him, we are cleansed by the redeeming blood of His Son.

In cultivating a marriage grounded in truth and vulnerability, we create an environment where forgiveness, understanding, and growth can flourish. By extending grace to one another and relying on the guidance of the Holy Spirit, we navigate the challenges of life together, continually drawing closer to God and to each other. It is within the refuge of a transparent and authentic relationship that we find healing, restoration, and the true fulfillment of the sacred covenant of marriage.

These reflections on intimacy, truth, and unity are only the beginning. In the next sections, we will continue to explore practical ways to live out these principles daily, nurturing a marriage that not only survives but thrives, anchored in the love and truth of Christ.

Surrendering and Humility

Testimony Excerpt

As our family expanded with the addition of more children, I observed that the kids would engage in intense debates over trivial matters. These discussions seemed to evoke a level of passion and intensity usually reserved for weighty topics like the financial collapse of a nation. I would watch in amazement as my children, with flushed faces and animated gestures, argued over who got the bigger slice of cake or whose turn it was to sit in the front seat of the car. In those moments, I saw a reflection of human nature—our inherent desire to be right, to be recognized, and to come out on top, even in the smallest of matters.

As a father, I took it upon myself to guide my children through these moments, not by forcing them to admit defeat but by encouraging them to choose love, mercy, and grace over the natural inclination to prove themselves right. I reminded them of the words in Ephesians 4:2, "Be completely humble and gentle; be patient, bearing with one another in love." I wanted them to understand that sometimes love means letting go of the need to win, and that true strength lies in humility and gentleness. Instead of viewing their siblings as adversaries, I encouraged them to see each other as teammates—each uniquely loved by God and deserving of respect and kindness.

I also emphasized the importance of humility in these situations, as the relentless pursuit of victory and being right only fueled conflict and was rooted in pride. Proverbs 13:10 tells us, "Where there is strife, there is pride, but wisdom is found in those who take advice." I explained to my children that pride often leads to unnecessary arguments and hurt feelings, while humility allows us to listen, to learn, and to grow. I tried to model this behavior for them, showing that it is okay to back down, to apologize, and to prioritize relationships over being right.

Although my efforts to instill these values in my children may not have been as successful as I had envisioned—as the arguments over the last piece of dessert still continued—I realized that perhaps the message was meant for me as well. Upon reflecting on this matter, I recognized how frequently I could have avoided unnecessary conflicts in discussions with my wife. My own pride often drove me to assert my correctness so strongly that I would even resort to drawing diagrams to illustrate my point, as if visual aids would somehow make my stance more valid. It was during this realization that I understood God was initiating a new transformative process in my life once again.

The Lord began to reveal to me that my desire to always be right was not only affecting my relationship with my wife but also hindering my spiritual growth. Philippians 2:3-4 came to mind: "Do nothing out of selfish ambition or vain conceit. Rather, in humility value others above yourselves, not looking to your own interests but each of you to the interests of the others." I had to acknowledge that my insistence on being right was often motivated by selfish ambition and a desire to elevate myself rather than build up my wife or strengthen our relationship. God was calling me to lay down my pride, to value my wife's perspective, and to approach our disagreements with a heart of humility.

This journey of transformation was not easy. It required me to swallow my pride and to recognize that being right was not as important as being loving. I had to learn to listen without preparing my rebuttal, to empathize rather than defend, and to seek unity over victory. It reminded me of James 1:19, which says, "My dear brothers and sisters, take note of this: Everyone should be quick to listen, slow to speak and slow to become angry." These words became my guide as I navigated moments of conflict, both with my children and with my wife.

Through this process, I began to see changes not only in myself but also in my family. My children, seeing me model humility and a willingness to admit when I was wrong, began to do the same. Slowly, the intensity of their arguments lessened, and moments of grace became more frequent. I realized that God was using my role as a father to teach me deeper lessons about His love, about the importance of humility, and about the kind of servant-hearted leadership that Christ exemplified. The transformation God was working in me was also being worked out in my family, and for that, I am truly grateful.

Surrendering and Humility

In my personal encounters, I have discovered that the concept of "bearing your cross" manifests itself in various forms and sizes. Referring to the scripture we previously discussed in Ephesians, Jesus exemplifies His love for His church by sacrificing His own life for it. He then calls upon men to emulate this selfless devotion for their wives. However, what does this truly entail? I have come to realize that it encompasses both significant gestures and subtle acts, each requiring us to humbly surrender and moderate ourselves.

When Jesus speaks of "bearing your cross" in Luke 9:23, He says, "Whoever wants to be my disciple must deny themselves and take up their cross daily and follow me." The act of bearing one's cross is not limited to grand displays of sacrifice, but it is found in the daily decisions to deny oneself for the sake of another. In marriage, this means putting our spouse's needs before our own, even in the small, seemingly inconsequential moments. It means choosing love when our pride demands recognition, and choosing humility when our ego craves validation.

The act of surrendering to Jesus stands as one of, if not the most crucial aspect of our ongoing spiritual growth. As we earnestly pursue Christ and endeavor to reflect His attributes, we commence a profound yet gradual transformation in our obedience to the Holy Spirit. Jesus provides a flawless illustration of surrender when He prays in the garden of Gethsemane. While beseeching the Father to spare Him from suffering, He ultimately surrenders and embraces the Father's will. In Matthew 26:38-42, we see Jesus' humanity and His divine obedience on full display.

Matthew 26:38-42 (NASB) "He said to them, 'My soul is deeply grieved, even to the point of death; remain here and keep watch with Me.' going a little farther, He fell face down and prayed, saying, 'My Father, if it is possible, let this cup pass from Me; yet not as I will, but as You will.' And He came to the disciples and found them sleeping, and said to Peter, 'So, you men could not keep watch with Me for one hour? Keep watching and praying, so that you do not come into temptation; the spirit is willing, but the flesh is weak.' He went away again a second time and prayed, saying, 'My Father, if this cup cannot pass away unless I drink it, Your will be done.'"

In this passage, Jesus demonstrates the ultimate act of surrender, a complete yielding of His desires to the will of the Father. This moment in Gethsemane is a powerful reminder that surrender is not always easy; it often comes with struggle, with the wrestling of our will against God's.

Yet, true surrender means trusting that God's plan is greater, even when it involves personal sacrifice. For us, as husbands, this means surrendering our will for the benefit of our wives and our families, trusting that God will use our sacrifices to bring about His perfect will.

Surrendering and making sacrifices for your spouse can manifest in seemingly small acts. It is in these moments that I truly capture the heart of my wife. For instance, when we both come home from work and settle down on the couch, if my wife asks me to fetch her a glass of water, I willingly oblige. Admittedly, my initial internal response may include a hint of confusion. I might wonder why I, despite being at a similar distance from the kitchen and having worked the same amount, am the one being asked to get the water. However, I remind myself of the importance of humility and proceed to retrieve her favorite cup, ensuring it is filled with the right amount of ice and bottled water, complete with her preferred metal straw.

It is in these small acts of service that we practice the selflessness that Jesus calls us to. Ephesians 5:25 tells us, "Husbands, love your wives, just as Christ loved the church and gave himself up for her." Christ's love for the church was marked by sacrifice, not just in the ultimate sense of the cross but in His daily acts of service, compassion, and love. When I choose to serve my wife in small ways, I am reflecting Christ's love for her, showing her that she is valued, cherished, and worthy of my time and effort.

These small moments of surrender and service may not seem significant, but they build the foundation of a strong marriage. They create an atmosphere of love and respect, where each partner feels valued and cared for. In doing so, we fulfill the call to bear our cross daily, to deny ourselves for the sake of another, and to love as Christ loved us. And in these moments, we experience the true joy of a Christ-centered marriage—one built on humility, sacrifice, and unconditional love.

This may appear trivial, but it is crucial to recognize that there are numerous instances where my wife sacrifices her comfort, energy, and time for my sake. Even if she didn't, would it demonstrate the character traits of God for me to spitefully ask her to get her own water? In what way have I surrendered in a Christ-like manner that teaches her about mercy and grace? Philippians 2:5-7 reminds us, "In your relationships with one another, have the same mindset as Christ Jesus: Who, being in very nature God, did not consider equality with God something to be used to his own advantage; rather, he made himself nothing by taking the very nature of a servant." The mindset of Christ is that of a servant, one who willingly humbles Himself for the sake of others. When we take on this mindset, even in the smallest actions, we reflect Christ's character to our spouse and to those around us.

Surrendering is an act filled with love and grace. During a disagreement, perhaps regarding something someone said, it is okay to be wrong, regardless of how convinced I am of being right. Being wrong does not diminish my worth; rather, surrendering becomes paramount because demonstrating the gracious and loving surrender of Jesus holds greater significance than being proven right. Proverbs 15:1 says, "A gentle answer turns away wrath, but a harsh word stirs up anger." Choosing gentleness, even when we feel justified in our anger, is a way to surrender our pride for the sake of peace. However, in discussions where it is crucial to correct or be accurate, it is important to stand firm while humbly correcting my spouse, setting aside pride in the process. This requires wisdom and discernment, which we are encouraged to seek from God, as James 1:5 tells us, "If any of you lacks wisdom, you should ask God, who gives generously to all without finding fault, and it will be given to you."

Matthew 16:24 (NASB) "Then Jesus said to His disciples, 'If anyone wants to come after Me, he must deny himself, take up his cross, and follow Me.'" Once again, we highlight the inherent connection between pursuing Jesus and the intimate bond of marriage. To follow Jesus, He instructs us to deny ourselves. Similarly, in our marriage, we must do the same, keeping in mind the greater purpose, which is to bring glory to God and fulfill His will. By humbling myself and preparing my soul for surrender, when necessary, to shower my wife with grace and mercy, I honor God and reflect His character. It is not about seeking recognition or expecting anything in return; it is about embodying the love of Christ, who gave Himself up for us without reservation or condition.

Marriage is an ongoing journey of learning how to lay down our lives for one another, as Christ did for the church. It is a journey that requires us to be intentional in our actions, to prioritize our spouse's needs, and to seek God's guidance in every aspect of our relationship. Ephesians 4:2-3 encourages us to "be completely humble and gentle; be patient, bearing with one another in love. Make every effort to keep the unity of the Spirit through the bond of peace." This unity is cultivated through the daily acts of surrender, the willingness to serve, and the grace we extend to one another. When we choose to deny ourselves and take up our cross in our marriage, we create a partnership that not only thrives but also glorifies God.

By consistently practicing surrender and selflessness, we lay the groundwork for a marriage that reflects the love of Christ. We are reminded that our actions, whether big or small, have the power to impact our spouse and our family profoundly. It is through these seemingly insignificant moments of sacrifice that we cultivate an environment where love, respect, and grace can flourish. In this way, we fulfill our calling as husbands to love our wives as Christ loved the church, and we experience the deep joy and fulfillment that comes from a marriage rooted in God's love and purpose.

Child Rearing

Testimony Excerpt

When the news of my wife's pregnancy reached us, an overwhelming sense of excitement coursed through my veins. The prospect of embarking on a new and thrilling adventure as a father filled me with anticipation, and I often found myself pondering the extent of my capabilities in this role. Given that I had never known the identity of my own father, it held great importance for me to transcend the shortcomings of my past and strive to become a superior man and father. I was determined to break the cycle, to offer my child the love, guidance, and stability that I had never experienced. The words of Psalm 68:5-6, which describe God as "a father to the fatherless," resonated deeply with me. I believed that if God could be my Father, He could also teach me to be a father to my own children.

Regrettably, my initial excitement and early encounters proved inadequate in steering my behavior towards the path of goodness. The arrival of my twin children coincided with my first year in the military, which inherently created a physical and emotional distance between us. As I succumbed to the influence of societal norms and battled substance abuse, I drifted further away from any semblance of responsible fatherhood. The combined weight of our marital troubles and my own foolish choices rendered me nearly invisible in the lives of my twins during their formative years. I found myself caught in the trap of pursuing worldly pleasures, forgetting the value of the blessings that God had given me. Proverbs 14:12 says, "There is a way that appears to be right, but in the end it leads to death." My path seemed to lead me away from the responsibilities I had as a husband and father, and I was blind to the damage I was causing.

Left with the weighty burden of raising our beautiful little boys, my faithful wife valiantly assumed the role of both mother and father. She was, in many ways, a reflection of God's unconditional love, enduring hardships and continuing to care for our children despite my failures. In hindsight, I trembled at the thought of the potential harm I had inflicted upon their development through my prolonged absence. Yet, by the grace of God, a divine call beckoned me towards His plan, granting me a golden opportunity to make a profound impact on their lives. I was reminded of the parable of the prodigal son (Luke 15:11-32), and I began to understand the depth of God's grace—that even when we stray, He welcomes us back with open arms, offering us another chance to make things right.

At that time, my way of life revolved around self-indulgence, prioritizing personal satisfaction above all else, regardless of the consequences for those around me. Parties and frivolous pursuits took precedence over embracing the responsibilities that come with being a father. Unsurprisingly, this only exacerbated the rift within my marriage, pushing us further apart. My wife, in her resilience, clung to hope, praying for a change that seemed impossible. Looking back, I now see her as a warrior of faith, embodying the spirit of 1 Corinthians 13:7: "Love bears all things, believes all things, hopes all things, endures all things."

However, my salvation through God's merciful grace marked a turning point in my life. It allowed me to share my transformative experience with my wife, who, in turn, embraced Christ as her savior. Instantly, my focus shifted towards healing our relationship, mending the lost time with our children, and immersing them in the teachings of the gospel. But this was just the beginning. Although we had found salvation, there were still countless aspects of life we needed to navigate, with parenting being a paramount challenge we faced. Philippians 1:6 gave us hope: "being confident of this, that he who began a good work in you will carry it on to completion until the day of Christ Jesus." We knew that God was not finished with us yet.

It was not until later that I discovered the greatest joy in mentoring and guiding my children as a father. As I delved deeper into my relationship with God, I began to unravel the true essence of fatherhood and being a true husband. I realized that fatherhood was not just about providing for my children's physical needs; it was about nurturing their hearts and souls, teaching them to walk in the ways of the Lord. Deuteronomy 6:6-7 became my guide: "These commandments that I give you today are to be on your hearts. Impress them on your children. Talk about them when you sit at home and when you walk along the road, when you lie down and when you get up."

Through this transformative process, I found the means to convey the profound impact of Christ's presence in my life, shaping the lives of my children with contextual wisdom and understanding. I began to see my role not just as a father, but as a shepherd, leading my children to the green pastures of God's love and truth. Psalm 23:1, "The Lord is my shepherd, I lack nothing," reminded me that God was my shepherd, guiding me, and I, in turn, was called to shepherd my children. The journey was not without its challenges, but each step forward was a testament to God's faithfulness, His ability to redeem what was broken, and His power to transform even the most wayward of hearts. By God's grace, I became the father I had always wanted to be—one who leads his children with love, patience, and unwavering faith.

Child Rearing

Having gained invaluable insights from my own experiences, if I were to offer advice to a man embarking on a young relationship with children on the way, I would emphasize that there is nothing more captivating to a mother than witnessing a father wholeheartedly embrace his responsibilities with unwavering love and determination. The act of stepping up and dutifully serving my family forged an immense bond not only with my children but also with my wife. By assuming the role of the father God had intended for me, I inadvertently called forth the very best from my wife. Proverbs 22:6 reminds us, "Start children off on the way they should go, and even when they are old they will not turn from it." My commitment to being present and nurturing our children created a ripple effect, prompting my wife to flourish in her role as a mother.

The example I set as a leader within our household compelled my family to join me on a collective journey of learning and growth, relieving my wife of the heavy burden of being the sole spiritual guide. Though her love for Jesus is fervent, her heart finds completeness in her husband's ability to guide and lead her. The joy that emanates from her is immeasurable when a father can confidently shepherd their children along the path of Christ. Ephesians 5:23 speaks of the husband as the head of the wife, just as Christ is the head of the church. This does not mean dominance, but rather a call to lead with love, humility, and sacrifice. When I stepped into my role as a spiritual leader, I could see the burden lifted from my wife's shoulders, and the peace that came from knowing she was not alone in raising our children in the faith.

3 John 1:4 (NASB) "I have no greater joy than this, to hear of my children walking in the truth." These words resonate deeply with me, as there is no greater satisfaction than knowing that my children are growing in their relationship with God. The absence of a father within the home undeniably inflicts profound harm upon the overall well-being of the family unit. Conversely, when a father, driven by his devotion to God, assumes his rightful place in the household, he becomes a beacon of structure and love for his family. Countless statistics serve as a stark reminder of the detrimental effects of fatherless homes, unveiling a distressing increase in issues such as suicide rates, incarceration durations, poverty levels, and the rampant abuse of substances like alcohol and drugs. Undoubtedly, this disheartening trend has become akin to a pervasive pandemic within the United States.

Yet, God has a different vision for the family. In Malachi 4:6, we read, "He will turn the hearts of the fathers to their children, and the hearts of the children to their fathers." God's desire is for fathers to be present, engaged, and active in their children's lives, creating a legacy of faith that can be passed down through generations. When I chose to turn my heart towards my children, I saw the impact it had—not just on them, but on the entire family dynamic. My wife's joy became evident, my children's sense of security grew, and our home became a place of peace, love, and spiritual growth.

The role of a father is not merely to provide financially or discipline when needed; it is a sacred calling to reflect the character of our Heavenly Father. It is about being present, guiding with wisdom, and loving unconditionally. Deuteronomy 1:31 reminds us of how God carries His children, "There you saw how the Lord your God carried you, as a father carries his son, all the way you went until you reached this place." I strive to carry my children in the same way—supporting, encouraging, and loving them every step of the way, even when the journey is challenging.

However, the essence of fatherhood transcends mere physical presence. As we have explored in previous chapters, our divine calling as fathers extends beyond the boundaries of mere existence. God beckons us to exemplify greatness as husbands, even to the extent of sacrificially laying down our lives for our wives, mirroring His own sacrifice for the Church. Furthermore, God's call extends to our role as fathers, urging us to become exceptional stewards of our children's lives. Thus, it is incumbent upon us not only to tend to their physical needs but also to nurture and shape their character. In this pursuit, we find guidance and inspiration in the example set by our heavenly Father, as exemplified in the words of Proverbs 4:11-12.

Proverbs 4:11-12 (NASB) "I have instructed you in the way of wisdom; I have led you in upright paths. When you walk, your steps will not be hampered; And if you run, you will not stumble."

Such is the wisdom and love that should flow from the heart of a devoted father, ever mindful of his responsibility to shape the lives of his children in accordance with God's divine blueprint. As fathers, we are called to be teachers and guides, imparting the wisdom of God and leading our children on the path of righteousness. This involves not only instruction but also exemplifying the values we wish to instill. Just as Proverbs 20:7 says, "The righteous lead blameless lives; blessed are their children after them." Our actions set the foundation upon which our children build their own lives of faith.

By actively embodying the qualities of a God-fearing father, we become agents of transformation within our families. We bring structure, stability, and unconditional love into our homes, creating an environment in which our children can thrive and flourish. Just as our heavenly Father serves as our ultimate role model, we, too, must strive to exemplify His teachings and principles, instilling them within the very fabric of our children's lives. Ephesians 6:4 urges fathers, "Do not exasperate your children; instead, bring them up in the training and instruction of the Lord." This verse challenges us to foster an atmosphere of love and encouragement, avoiding harshness, and instead nurturing our children in the ways of God.

Through our unwavering commitment to God's guidance, we become vessels of His grace, ensuring that our children walk upon the path of wisdom, righteousness, and everlasting joy. It is not an easy task, and we will face challenges along the way, but we can rest in the knowledge that

God is with us every step. Isaiah 41:10 provides reassurance: "So do not fear, for I am with you; do not be dismayed, for I am your God. I will strengthen you and help you; I will uphold you with my righteous right hand."

Nurturing the character of your child is a task that demands both care and wisdom. Drawing mostly from my experience of raising boys, as they outnumber my lone little girl, I have come to understand the importance of imparting wisdom that resonates deep within their souls. Mere words of caution may fall short in shaping their character, which is why it is crucial for us, as fathers, to seek our own understanding and wisdom. Proverbs 2:6 tells us, "For the Lord gives wisdom; from his mouth come knowledge and understanding." We must seek God's wisdom to guide our children effectively. By doing so, we can present these insights to our children in a manner that contextualizes their application in real-life situations, making God's truth tangible and relevant to their young minds.

For instance, if we aim to instill values such as respect, honor, and duty in our children, we must go beyond mere obligation. Instead, we should ignite within them a genuine desire to embody these virtues. This involves recognizing and calling forth the potential for greatness within our boys, while also nurturing the qualities of strength, integrity, and honor within our girl. The book of Proverbs offers timeless wisdom for guiding our children, reminding us in Proverbs 22:15 that "Folly is bound up in the heart of a child, but the rod of discipline will drive it far away." Discipline is not just about correction, but also about instilling discipline in a way that inspires our children to embrace righteousness willingly.

However, calling our children to ideals such as duty and responsibility can be challenging. After all, which child truly desires the weight of responsibility or the burden of obligation? As fathers, we must skillfully develop their character, taking into account their unique personalities and inclinations. Children often respond positively to attention and rewards, so when they demonstrate behavior that aligns with the wisdom we have imparted, it is important to recognize and reward them with our sincere praise. Proverbs 3:27 says, "Do not withhold good from those to whom it is due, when it is in your power to act." Acknowledging our children's good behavior and efforts helps reinforce those positive traits, allowing them to flourish.

Teaching duty and responsibility requires finesse. We must convince our children that there is greater fulfillment and reward in pursuing long-term goals rather than succumbing to immediate desires. It is a gradual process, taking baby steps and allowing them to witness the tangible benefits in the short term. Romans 5:3-4 reminds us that "suffering produces perseverance; perseverance, character; and character, hope." This process of character development may not always be easy, but it ultimately yields a deeper sense of purpose and hope in our children. As they begin to grasp the concept and appreciate the significance of their actions, we can guide them towards setting higher goals and embracing noble ideals.

A biblical story that beautifully illustrates the concept of responsibility is the parable of the master and the talents found in Matthew 25:14-30. In this parable, the servants who used their talents wisely were rewarded, while the one who hid his talent out of fear was reprimanded. By sharing this story with our children, we can teach them the importance of using their gifts and fulfilling their responsibilities, not just for personal gain but for the glory of God. By encouraging our children to seek to please God, we witness the manifestation of our wisdom within them, as they learn to serve with love and diligence.

Being a conscientious man and diligently developing our children in a similar manner has a profound impact on the unity of the family unit as a whole. Presenting ourselves as parents with intent, dedicating ourselves to the honor and growth of our children in the ways of the Lord, not only strengthens the bond between husband and wife, but also serves as a unifying force. Marriage entails sharing ideals and goals, and by focusing on the family as a cohesive entity, fostering wisdom and mercy, we lay yet another foundation for growth firmly rooted in truth. Ecclesiastes 4:12 states, "Though one may be overpowered, two can defend themselves. A cord of three strands is not quickly broken." When husband, wife, and God are united in purpose, the family becomes an unbreakable force for good.

As fathers, we must continually strive to reflect God's love and wisdom to our children. By being intentional in nurturing their character, teaching them about responsibility, and guiding them towards God's truth, we create an environment where our children can grow to be strong, faithful, and resilient. This is the legacy we leave—a family built upon the solid foundation of God's word, where love, grace, and wisdom flow abundantly.

If I Could Change One Thing

Testimony Excerpt

Prior to my marriage, I actively sought the company of various women, engaging in behavior that revolved around satisfying my own desires without considering the potential consequences. I had honed special techniques to attract women purely for my own pleasure, unwittingly creating an expectation of instant gratification. I was living a life that lacked true purpose, driven by the fleeting fulfillment of my own lusts. Proverbs 14:12 says, "There is a way that appears to be right, but in the end it leads to death." I was blinded by my pursuits, unaware of the deep emptiness that awaited me on that path.

However, once I entered into matrimony, I grappled internally with an ongoing desire to seek out other women. It wasn't because my wife lacked anything, but rather because I had developed a distorted sense of needing new encounters beyond the confines of a committed partnership. My past had conditioned me to believe that the only way to feel fulfilled was through constant novelty. This struggle brought to mind James 1:14-15: "But each person is tempted when they are dragged away by their own evil desire and enticed. Then, after desire has conceived, it gives birth to sin; and sin, when it is full-grown, gives birth to death." My unchecked desires were becoming a source of internal conflict that threatened to destroy my marriage.

Regrettably, this mindset eventually led me down a path of addiction to pornography, which persisted for a decade before I could break free from its grip. Pornography provided the illusion of satisfaction without the real intimacy that God intended for marriage. It was a counterfeit version of the love that I should have been cultivating with my wife. Throughout this struggle, I attempted to conceal my addiction from my spouse, but inevitably, she would discover the truth, forcing me to repeatedly apologize and reaffirm my dedication to our relationship. The consequences of my actions introduced tension into our home, reawakening past wounds and causing my wife to doubt and mistrust. The enemy used my secrecy and deceit to create division, and I was reminded of John 10:10, where Jesus warns, "The thief comes only to steal and kill and destroy." The enemy was attempting to steal the joy and unity from our marriage.

Thankfully, our God is abundant in mercy and grace, and so is my spouse. My wife embodied the spirit of 1 Corinthians 13:7: "Love bears all things, believes all things, hopes all things, endures all things." Through her unwavering love and forgiveness, she gave me hope that there was still a way forward for us. Through a steadfast commitment to studying and seeking God, I was ultimately able to conquer this immense obstacle. I came to understand the importance of true repentance—turning away from sin and towards God. Acts 3:19 says, "Repent, then, and turn to God, so that your sins may be wiped out, that times of refreshing may come from the Lord." I longed for that refreshing, for the freedom that could only come from God.

It was the realization of God's blessings upon my life and my involvement in His ministry that fueled my desire for lasting change. I began to recognize that my addiction was not just harming my marriage, but also hindering my ability to serve God fully. Romans 6:12-14 reminded me, "Therefore do not let sin reign in your mortal body so that you obey its evil desires. Do not offer any part of yourself to sin as an instrument of wickedness, but rather offer yourselves to God." I knew I needed to surrender every part of myself to God, including my desires, so that I could be an instrument of His righteousness.

By embracing God's transformative power and grace, I found the strength to overcome my destructive patterns and break free from the stronghold of addiction. It wasn't an overnight transformation; it was a daily decision to submit to God's will and resist the enemy's lies. James 4:7 says, "Submit yourselves, then, to God. Resist the devil, and he will flee from you." Through prayer, accountability, and God's Word, I gradually saw the chains of addiction break. The healing process brought restoration to my marriage and allowed my wife to witness the profound impact of God's work in my life. The walls of mistrust slowly began to come down, and we started rebuilding our relationship on the foundation of truth and grace.

Through His unfailing love and the unwavering support of my spouse, I was able to leave behind my past mistakes and embark on a new chapter filled with hope, redemption, and a renewed commitment to living in accordance with God's plan. 2 Corinthians 5:17 encapsulates this journey: "Therefore, if anyone is in Christ, the new creation has come: The old has gone, the new is here!" I became a new creation, no longer defined by my past sins, but by the redemptive power of God's grace. Today, my marriage stands as a testament to the power of God's love and forgiveness. It is my prayer that my story can serve as a beacon of hope for others who may be struggling, that they too may find freedom in Christ and experience the joy of true intimacy that comes from walking in His light.

If I Could Change One Thing

Throughout our lives, it is common for us to reflect on the choices we've made and ponder what we would alter if given the chance. Like many others, I carry a burden of regrets and experience a profound sense of shame over certain aspects of my past. However, in those moments, I must remind myself that God often selects the lowly and weak to showcase the incredible strength found in His saving grace. 1 Corinthians 1:27 tells us, "But God chose the foolish things of the world to shame the wise; God chose the weak things of the world to shame the strong." It is within this context that I wish to delve into a contemplation specifically centered around my marriage and the reasons behind it.

If I had the opportunity to change just one aspect of my marriage, it would be to have never engaged in any form of intimacy with other women before entering into the sacred bond of matrimony. While this may appear to be a simple desire, it is deeply rooted in the far-reaching psychological and spiritual consequences that accompany such choices. Sexual intimacy is a sacred act that God designed to be shared exclusively within the covenant of marriage, and stepping outside of that divine plan brings with it a host of unintended repercussions. Hebrews 13:4 states, "Marriage should be honored by all, and the marriage bed kept pure, for God will judge the adulterer and all the sexually immoral." I have come to understand the profound wisdom behind this command, as the consequences of my past actions have impacted my marriage in ways I could never have anticipated.

By acknowledging the impact of my past actions on my marriage, I hope to unravel the intricate layers of consequences that have influenced our relationship. The emotional baggage of past relationships, the unrealistic expectations, and the shame that came from my choices all contributed to creating barriers between my wife and me. It is through the lens of biblical teachings and personal introspection that I aim to bring forth a deeper understanding of the challenges we have faced and the transformative power of God's Word. Psalm 51:10 became my prayer: "Create in me a pure heart, O God, and renew a steadfast spirit within me." I knew that in order to fully embrace the covenant of marriage as God intended, I needed a heart that was cleansed and renewed by Him.

The reality is that our past actions have consequences, but the beauty of God's grace is that He can redeem even the most broken parts of our lives. Joel 2:25 promises, "I will repay you for the years the locusts have eaten." Though I cannot change my past, I have witnessed God restore what was lost and bring beauty from ashes. My hope is that by sharing these reflections, others may understand the importance of honoring God's design for intimacy and experience the freedom that comes from living within His will.

For it is within the realms of vulnerability and self-reflection that true growth can occur. By sharing my experiences and insights, I hope to encourage others who may be grappling with similar struggles to seek solace in the unending love and forgiveness offered by our Heavenly Father. Together, let us embark on a journey of self-discovery and healing, guided by the profound wisdom found within the pages of Scripture. The more we open our hearts to God's truth, the more we allow His transforming power to shape our lives. Vulnerability is not a sign of weakness but a sign of strength, for it is in our weakness that God's power is made perfect (2 Corinthians 12:9).

1 Corinthians 7:1-5 (NASB) "Now concerning the things about which you wrote, it is good for a man not to touch a woman. But because of sexual immoralities, each man is to have his own wife, and each woman is to have her own husband. The husband must fulfill his duty to his wife, and likewise the wife also to her husband. The wife does not have authority over her own body, but the husband does; and likewise the husband also does not have authority over his own body, but the wife does. Stop depriving one another, except by agreement for a time so that you may

devote yourselves to prayer, and come together again so that Satan will not tempt you because of your lack of self-control."

First and foremost, abstaining from sexual activity until marriage is an act of honoring God. By choosing to remain celibate, we acknowledge the divine intention behind God's creation and seek to glorify Him. Throughout history, sexual immorality has plagued humanity, but by refraining from intimacy before marriage, we create a space for God to pour out His blessings upon our union. This act of obedience serves as a testimony to others, as we openly declare our allegiance to Jesus, and in turn, He acknowledges us before the Father (Matthew 10:32). Through this deliberate choice, our hearts become more attuned to the will of God, preparing us for His divine plan to unfold in our lives. Proverbs 3:5-6 encourages us to "Trust in the Lord with all your heart and lean not on your own understanding; in all your ways submit to him, and he will make your paths straight." Trusting in God's plan for intimacy, even when the world says otherwise, allows us to experience the fullness of His design for our relationships.

The consequences of engaging in premarital sex weigh heavily on the minds and hearts of individuals, even those who do not profess faith. Despite fulfilling the deceptive desires propagated by the evil one, individuals often offer countless justifications for indulging in sexual acts, disregarding the potential harm to their own mental and spiritual well-being. Engaging in sexual relationships with multiple partners directly impacts how we perceive and accept our future spouse, even before intimacy is shared with them. The emotional scars and unrealistic expectations create barriers that hinder true intimacy within the marriage covenant. Paul writes in 1 Corinthians 6:18, "Flee from sexual immorality. All other sins a person commits are outside the body, but whoever sins sexually, sins against their own body." This warning serves as a reminder of the lasting impact that sexual sin has on our lives, not just physically, but emotionally and spiritually as well.

By striving to honor God with our bodies and our relationships, we create an environment where His blessings can flow freely. As we reflect on our past mistakes, it is essential to remember that God is not only a God of justice but also a God of grace and redemption. No matter how far we have strayed, His arms are always open to welcome us back, offering us a fresh start and the opportunity to walk in His truth. The healing and restoration that come from submitting our lives to God are beyond anything we could achieve on our own. Psalm 147:3 tells us, "He heals the brokenhearted and binds up their wounds."

In the pursuit of becoming experienced or skilled in sexual matters, some individuals may believe that engaging in intercourse before marriage is necessary. However, this belief is false. Consider this perspective: If you and your spouse have abstained from sexual relations until marriage, your union becomes the pinnacle of your experiences, making your partner the greatest you have ever encountered, and vice versa. The beauty of waiting is that the intimacy shared within the sacred bond of marriage is incomparable, untainted by past experiences or comparisons. Hebrews 13:4 declares, "Marriage should be honored by all, and the marriage bed kept pure, for God will judge the adulterer and all the sexually immoral." The purity of waiting allows the marriage bed to be a place of honor, free from the baggage of previous relationships.

However, having engaged in sexual relationships with multiple partners, one begins to compare their spouse's performance to past experiences, which is inherently unfair. It creates unrealistic expectations and fosters discontentment, which ultimately harms the marriage. God, being all-knowing, has predestined us for His church and good works. By defiling ourselves before marriage, we risk forfeiting some of the blessings that were meant for us in the sacred consummation of the spouse God has placed in our lives. Moreover, we find ourselves in a position where we are comparing the precious gift provided by God to the fleeting pleasures offered by the world. Romans 12:2 urges us, "Do not conform to the pattern of this world, but be transformed by the renewing of your mind." We must renew our minds and reject the world's lies about intimacy in order to fully embrace the beauty of God's design for marriage.

In acknowledging the profound impact of our past actions, we can now embark on a journey of healing and restoration. By seeking forgiveness and embracing God's grace, we can surrender our past mistakes and open ourselves to the fullness of God's blessings within the sanctity of marriage. 1 John 1:9 reassures us, "If we confess our sins, he is faithful and just and will forgive us our sins and purify us from all unrighteousness." Through confession and repentance, we can be purified, allowing us to experience the deep connection and intimacy that God intended for marriage. Let us humbly walk in the light of His truth, recognizing the value and significance of reserving sexual intimacy for the covenant of marriage.

The prevailing culture of our day encourages men to pursue multiple partners, perpetuating a psychological pattern rooted in the constant quest for new and exciting experiences with each encounter. This insatiable desire for novelty is precisely why pornography can be so damaging, as it offers an endless array of stimulating experiences with each visit, distorting our perception and solidifying a false reality. Proverbs 27:20 says, "Death and Destruction are never satisfied, and neither are human eyes." The endless pursuit of satisfaction through multiple partners or pornography is a cycle that leads to emptiness and destruction, as it can never truly fulfill the desires of the heart.

It is reasonable to speculate that men who have had a higher number of previous partners are also more prone to infidelity, driven by the allure of seeking the dopamine rush that comes with new experiences. The enemy uses these desires to pull men away from the commitment and covenant they have made with their spouse. Proverbs 5:18-19 encourages us to "rejoice in the wife of your youth" and to let her love satisfy us always. By focusing on the beauty and uniqueness of the relationship God has given us, we can resist the temptation to seek fulfillment elsewhere. When we align our hearts with God's truth and seek satisfaction in His design for intimacy, we find true joy and fulfillment that is not dependent on novelty but rather on the steadfast commitment and love that grows deeper over time. The joy that comes from honoring God's design is enduring, untainted by comparisons or fleeting experiences, and allows us to experience the true depth of intimacy as He intended.

However, by choosing to remain celibate, we deliberately disrupt the development of unhealthy physical and psychological habits. We purposefully reserve ourselves for a greater and more profound satisfaction that awaits us in the arms of our chosen spouse. This act of delaying gratification grants us invaluable insight and cultivates a deep sense of gratitude when the time comes for our desires to be fulfilled. By sacrificing our immediate urges for the sake of a long-term goal, the eventual experience is magnified in its significance and joy. Galatians 6:9 encourages us, "Let us not become weary in doing good, for at the proper time we will reap a harvest if we do not give up." The harvest we reap by waiting is a deeper, more meaningful connection that honors God's plan for our lives.

If given the opportunity to change just one thing from my past, I would wholeheartedly choose to honor God by refraining from seeking sexual encounters with anyone until the Father revealed to me the spouse He had preordained for me. In making this choice, I would honor God in His divine creation, recognizing and embracing the sanctity and intention behind the gift of sexuality. By abstaining from premarital intimacy, I would safeguard myself against false judgments and comparisons towards my future spouse, ensuring that our connection is built on trust, authenticity, and the purest expression of love. Moreover, this intentional choice to honor God's plan for sexual intimacy fosters healthy habits and establishes godly ordinances within the sacred bond of marriage. Ephesians 5:3 reminds us, "But among you there must not be even a hint of sexual immorality, or of any kind of impurity, or of greed, because these are improper for God's holy people." Abstaining from sexual immorality allows us to set a firm foundation for a marriage that is pleasing to God.

In embracing this path, we open ourselves to the fullness of God's blessings and experience the beauty of a loving, intimate relationship that is rooted in His divine design. God desires for us to experience the joy of a pure and committed love, one that reflects His unwavering love for us. Let us, therefore, commit ourselves to walking in purity, guided by the wisdom and grace of our Heavenly Father, and rejoice in the abundant fulfillment that awaits us when we honor His principles and follow His lead. Psalm 37:4 says, "Take delight in the Lord, and he will give you the desires of your heart." By delighting in God's ways and trusting in His timing, we can rest assured that He will fulfill the deepest desires of our hearts in ways far greater than we could ever imagine.

Conclusion

In the first section, we explored my personal testimony, sharing the journey from meeting my future wife at a young age to the many challenges we faced as young parents and the separation we endured while I served in the military. I also shared my struggles with substance abuse and the transformative experience I had during my time in prison. This was a season of introspection—one in which I came to understand my own role in the problems that had affected my life. It was here that I sought not only external help but also a deeper, spiritual intervention that could truly transform my heart and mind. Ultimately, it was through salvation in Jesus Christ that I found hope, and through a growing relationship with Him, I was led to reconciliation with my wife and the restoration of our marriage. We wanted to share this story not just as a testimony of our own lives but as an inspiration for others, offering hope that no matter the depth of our struggles, God's transformative love can bring redemption and healing.

The concept of "one flesh" in marriage is foundational to understanding God's design for the sacred union between husband and wife. Rooted in the biblical account of Adam and Eve, this concept signifies the deep unity and oneness that extends far beyond physical connection—it is emotional, spiritual, and relational. The creation of woman from Adam's rib illustrates the intimate and inseparable bond intended by God. When a man and woman enter the covenant of marriage, they become "one flesh," forming a partnership designed to reflect the divine. This union demands responsibility, selflessness, and an unwavering commitment to care for each other as they would for their own bodies. Scripture teaches that husbands are to love their wives as Christ loved the church, and by embracing this "one flesh" concept, couples can cultivate a thriving bond that honors God's original design for marriage.

We also discussed the personal pursuit of Jesus within the context of marriage. Often, we are taught that marriage is a fifty-fifty partnership, but this notion can be misleading. True, lasting marriage requires a wholehearted, 100% commitment from both spouses. When we view marriage as a covenant where each person is fully committed regardless of circumstances, we create an environment where grace flourishes. In a

Christ-centered marriage, the focus shifts from seeking fulfillment in one another to finding true fulfillment in God. This reorients our hearts, allowing us to cover each other's shortcomings with mercy, to see disagreements through the lens of grace, and to find resolution through prayer rather than pride. By individually pursuing Jesus, spouses are better equipped to support, encourage, and pray for each other, which creates a foundation that is unshakable.

To build a healthy and Christ-centered marriage, we must prioritize our relationship with God above all else, seeking Him daily and creating opportunities to grow spiritually together. As each spouse embarks on their own journey with Christ, they become more capable of offering the love, grace, and patience needed within their marriage. This pursuit of Jesus is what ultimately equips us to face life's challenges with hope and confidence, knowing that God's plan is good.

One of my favorite chapters in our journey together has been "Live in Truth." Living in truth is foundational to our relationship with God and with each other. Jesus Himself taught that true worship must be in spirit and in truth. As we strive to live in truth, we allow ourselves to be transformed, shedding layers of shame and pretense. Ephesians 5 calls husbands to love their wives as Christ loved the church, a sacrificial love that leads to sanctification. Walking in the light, as mentioned in 1 John 1:7, allows for fellowship with God and freedom from sin. Truth and vulnerability go hand in hand, creating an environment where intimacy can flourish. When we share our struggles, seek forgiveness, and extend grace to our spouse, we cultivate a relationship that reflects God's deep love for us. In transparency and authenticity, we find the true fulfillment that the sacred covenant of marriage was always intended to bring.

Bearing our cross in marriage means surrendering ourselves daily—laying down our pride, our desires, and even our need to be right. Jesus modeled ultimate surrender in the garden of Gethsemane, and we too are called to surrender for the sake of our marriage. Whether it's through small acts of service or choosing humility in the midst of conflict, each sacrifice we make for our spouse is an act of worship to God. Recognizing the sacrifices our spouse makes for us and responding with gratitude and love reflects the character of Jesus. Surrender isn't weakness; it's a powerful expression of love and an essential part of reflecting God's character in our marriage.

Embracing fatherhood has also been a significant part of my journey. True fatherhood goes beyond simply being present—it involves sacrificially laying down one's life for the sake of the family, leading with love, and shaping the hearts of our children. A father's role as the spiritual leader of the home brings stability, love, and joy not only to the children but also to the mother. Fatherlessness, on the other hand, has profound negative effects on families and society at large. As fathers, we are called to nurture the character of our children, instill in them a love for God, and teach them the values of respect, honor, and responsibility. By embodying these values ourselves, we provide an example for our children to follow, and we create an environment where they can grow in wisdom and grace. When we are God-fearing parents, we strengthen not only our family unit but also lay the foundation for future generations to live in the truth of God's love.

Finally, we reflected on our past choices and the regrets that have shaped us. Choosing to abstain from premarital intimacy is a way of honoring God's design, and it creates space for His blessings in marriage. Engaging in premarital sexual relationships can leave scars that affect future relationships, but God's grace is greater than our past mistakes. By choosing purity and seeking forgiveness, we create an environment in which love can flourish, unencumbered by comparisons or regrets. Honoring God in this way safeguards our marriage, building trust, intimacy, and love that reflects His divine plan. Embracing purity isn't just about what we avoid; it's about what we gain—God's blessings, a deeper connection with our spouse, and the joy that comes from knowing we are walking in His will.

In conclusion, my hope and prayer are that through the testimony we have shared and the lessons God has taught us, you are now better equipped to pursue a beautiful, Christ-centered marriage in your own life. Marriage is not always easy; it requires perseverance, sacrifice, and most importantly, the grace of God. But it is also a beautiful journey that, when centered on Christ, reflects the very heart of God's love for His people. I pray that you find strength in God's Word, hope in His promises, and joy in His presence. May our story serve as a beacon of hope for you, a reminder that God is always in the business of redemption, and that no matter where you've been, He has a plan for your future. May you seek Him first in all things, trust in His timing, and honor Him in every aspect of your relationship. And may you experience the profound joy and fulfillment that comes from a marriage rooted in His love.

Made in the USA
Columbia, SC
17 November 2024